Our Passion, God's Power accurately and effectively illustrates the importance of two distinct yet inseparable factors. In an era plagued with compromise, gaining a fresh, Biblical perspective on passion is a necessary component for revival. This is an essential read for Christians around the globe.

> – Zeke Lam, author of *subMISSION*
> and founder of Submission Ministries

OUR PASSION,
GOD'S
POWER

Adam Meisberger

CROSSBOOKS
PUBLISHING

CrossBooks™
A Division of LifeWay
1663 Liberty Drive
Bloomington, IN 47403
www.crossbooks.com
Phone: 1-866-879-0502

First published by CrossBooks 06/25/2013

ISBN: 978-1-4627-2926-5 (sc)
ISBN: 978-1-4627-2928-9 (hc)
ISBN: 978-1-4627-2927-2 (e)

Library of Congress Control Number: 2013911499

Printed in the United States of America.

This book is printed on acid-free paper.

To all desiring more of Jesus

TABLE OF CONTENTS

PREFACE

We only get one life upon this earth. We get one opportunity to make much of our lives—to live as God desires. But in what way does God intend for us to live?

Too many Christians are giving in to a powerless religion. Not being able to break old sinful habits. Constantly existing in a state of joylessness and anxiety. Seeing very little fruit produced. Acting as if loved ones will never change for the better.

Where is the power of God among His people in our day? Why are so many Christians living defeated lives and acting as if nothing will ever change? We are living in dangerous and scary times. Christians are growing cold and losing faith in the truth. Something needs to change. We are in great need of Christians everywhere to begin experiencing God's power in a way like never before. But for this to happen, something needs to transform within the heart of every believer. And that is the reason for this book.

"Blessed are those who hunger and thirst for righteousness, for they will be filled."

—Jesus in Matthew 5:6

"It is not enough to be evangelical in faith and heart; we must be utterly possessed by Christ, utterly impassioned by His love and grace, utterly ablaze with His power and glory. Every earthly part of our being, in the words of the great hymn, must glow with God's fire divine. The wood is not enough, the alter is not enough, the sacrifice is not enough—we need the fire! Fire of God, descend upon us anew! Set us ablaze, Lord, set us ablaze!"[1]

—Wesley L. Duewel

INTRODUCTION

More to This Life

"I believe, and I could be wrong here but I do not think I am, that God's people are hungry for the real spiritual food. They have had it with artificial light and hard, stale bread and odorless incense. They have had it with cheap imitations imported from the world; they long for the reality of God's presence among them."[2]

- A.W. Tozer

Have you ever thought to yourself, *"There has got to be more to life than this?"* I know I have. Let me be clear, I understand Scripture speaks that we should be content regardless of our circumstances, such as in Philippians 4:11 where the apostle Paul states, "I have learned in whatever state I am, to be content." However, I truly believe this feeling of wanting more out of our lives is from God and that He puts this desire within our hearts because He actually has more that He wants us, as His people, to be experiencing.

There is a vital difference between being content with whatever God brings our way, verses being content with the results of a life lived in sin, disobedience and unbelief. If we are living lives pleasing to God, then no matter in what circumstances we find ourselves, our contentment should be in God alone, regardless of whether we have wealth or poverty, expensive clothes or rags, good health or an incurable disease, a safe and comfortable home or a dangerous and inhospitable place to live. Whatever God desires to give us in this life we must be able to receive it all with joy as we trust Him.[3]

Yet, there are certain areas in our lives with which we must never be content. We must never be content living in disbelief, walking in the flesh instead of the Spirit, lacking desire and passion for the things of God, showing no sign of transformation in our lives, continuing to struggle with the same old sins time and time again and so forth. Being content while failing to walk in the transformational power of God in our daily lives is not the contentedness God desires for us and will ultimately result in a powerless, apathetic life. If we are content with our lives remaining the same while there is revealed sin within us then we are being careless and apathetic, and we are committing the sin of Sodom of which God rebukes the people of Jerusalem in Ezekiel 16:49-50, "Now this was the sin of your sister Sodom: She and her daughters were arrogant, overfed and unconcerned; they did not help the poor and needy. They were haughty and did detestable things before me. Therefore I did away with them as you have seen."

The apostle Paul was able to rightly say he had learned to be content no matter his circumstance because he knew he was being the man God wanted him to be and doing exactly what God desired him to do. Therefore, Paul was content whether in comfort or discomfort, safety or danger. His primary concern was to live a life that glorified God. We, likewise, should only be content when our lives are bringing glory to God.

Now, let us go back to the concept of there being *more to life* for a moment. Often a person has a desire for something more to their life and attempts to fill this desire by buying something new, pursuing after a new hobby, getting a new job, starting a new ministry, earning more money or beginning a new relationship. However, trying to fulfill our desire for more to life through some temporal and fleeting change, pleasure or joy will never satisfy us. Rather this desire should lead us to the source which will ultimately result in our experiencing true and lasting transformation, pleasure and joy.

Too often we assume that normalcy in our lives is a good thing. We may consider our usual life experience and believe that this is just how life is and that there is not any more to life than the same old, same old. We may even think that those who hunger and thirst for something more to life are unreasonable, foolish dreamers and wishful thinkers. Sometimes we as Christians say things such as, *"I am content with everything in my life just as it is, as the Bible says I should be,"* yet we continue to struggle with the same patterns of sin, continue to waste much of our time doing things of no eternal value and continue to have an apathetic approach towards prayer and reading the Bible. We may say we are content with life, yet we allow ourselves to be driven by anxiety, stress, depression and worry. Other times we may say we are content with life but in the same breath say, *"I know I am not fully surrendering my life to the Lord."* Or maybe we recognize that our lives reflect a greater passion for pursuing the things of this world than for pursuing the things of God.

As a pastor, I am afforded the privilege of talking with a variety of people about the Lord while knowing the pure joy of being called to teach and preach the truth of God's word to His Church. At the same time, the longer I am in the ministry, the more the Lord opens my eyes to something extremely heartbreaking among so many people who confess His name. Something is missing among an alarming number of those who confess to be Christians. What is missing?

The answer in one word—PASSION. Not just any old passion but an undying and full-fledged passion, hunger and thirst for the things of God, specifically, for Jesus Christ.

It is likely for us who live in Western culture, particularly in the United States of America, that we would not label the majority of professing Christians we know as being passionate for the things of God. But before we begin pointing our fingers, we must ask ourselves, *"Am I really all that passionate for the things of God?"* Perhaps we prefer to think about ourselves—*"Yes, I am very passionate about the things of God. I go to church, I read . . . well, I try to read my Bible every day, I pray, I've been baptized. God is the most important thing in my life!"* All of these things are good, but are not necessarily evidence of our being passionate for the things of God. We may attempt to convince others that our hearts burn for the things of God because we want that to be true. However, saying what we want to be true about our lives is quite different than actually living out that truth.

It is easy for us as Christians to convince ourselves we are passionate for God for this reason—we have defined, for ourselves, what it is to be passionate for God. If there is no clear definition of what it means to be passionate for God, then we can easily say, *"Yes, I am passionate for God."* Yet, in examining the condition of countless churches across the Western world, it does not appear that the majority of Christians burn for the things of God. Certain studies reveal that there is little or no difference between the lives of Christians and non-Christians—in behavior, thinking, entertainment, morals, rebelliousness, sexual immorality, divorce, abuse, lying, cheating, stealing, envy.[4] In one interview, the president of the Barna Research Group, said, "When we look at the values, lifestyles, the moral perspective and behaviors of Christians, we can see that there's virtually no difference between Christians and non-Christians."[5] In a *Christian Today* article there is a convicting quote by a man on the Barna Group research team, "The respect, patience, self-control and kindness of born-again Christians should astound people, but the lifestyles and relationships of born-again believers are not much different than others."[6]

Now we are getting to the reason for this book. God has been burning this concept of PASSION on my heart for some time now, and this burning keeps getting hotter and hotter. Often I feel as Jeremiah when he says God's word "is in my heart like a fire, a fire shut up in my bones. I am weary of holding it in; indeed, I cannot" (Jeremiah 20:9). Likewise, I can no longer hold in this burning.

I would ask each reader to please carefully weigh everything in this book with Scripture, for I am only a man, and in and of myself can err. Admittedly, I do not have everything figured out. Not at all! I simply want to bring out the truth of God's word, especially those truths which are not being displayed in the lives of so many professing Christians in our day. For this reason, I write this book, because I know that there is more to this Christian life than what so many of us are currently experiencing.

The specific verse God laid upon my heart as the focal point is Matthew 5:6, "Blessed are those who hunger and thirst for righteousness, for they shall be filled." I feel a strong urgency in my spirit regarding the message I am going to share. I am convinced we are living in perilous times. These times demand that people begin stepping up and speaking the truth. There is little time left. The apostle Paul warned Timothy, "But mark this: there will be terrible times in the last days" (2 Timothy 3:1). Paul then goes on to describe how people will behave in the last days—that there will be those who have a form of godliness but who also deny its power.[7] I believe we are seeing this evidence displayed in our day, especially among professing Christians of the Western world.

Some may wonder how this concept of passion and power fit together. In this book, I will try my best, with the aide of the Holy Spirit, to explain how a lack of passion for the Lord is leading to a lack of power among Christians. The truths of Scripture reveal that there is substantially more to life than what the majority of us are experiencing. And I would argue it has to do with our passion for righteousness, or more to the point, our lack of a passion for righteousness.

As you read the words of this book, pray that the Lord softens your heart and opens your eyes to reveal how this message might apply to you personally, to your church and to Christians all around you. And as He does, also pray that He empower you to act in accordance with His truth.

"Heavenly Father, I pray, anoint the pages of this book with Your Spirit. Soften the heart of each and every individual who reads the following words. Open the eyes of the blind. May the deaf hear for the first time. May the dead come to life. Speak to each one, Lord. Ignite in each heart a passion, hunger and thirst for You, for righteousness. Through Your power, make all who read the words of this book more like Jesus Christ. Amen."

1

Desperate for Water and Food

"God's holy fire only descends upon prepared, obedient, hungry hearts. Perhaps the need that underlies all needs is that we are not hungry enough, not thirsty enough, not whole-souled enough in our desire."[8]

- Wesley L. Duewel

We've all been thirsty before, but the question is—how thirsty? Though I have never been thirsty to the point that I thought I was going to die, I have experienced a desperate thirst. I can recall going on a hike in the woods with my family when I was just a little boy. It was a hot day and an intense hike from what I can remember, at least from a boy's perspective. As a boy of only about nine or ten years of age, my short legs wore out easily. I do not remember too much about that day, but one thing I do remember is the thirst I had. We were headed back to the car and all I could think about was getting a drink. My mouth was dryer than sawdust and I was desperate for water. I could hardly wait for the moment I would arrive at the car, take hold of the jug of water, and have my thirst wonderfully quenched.

Dying of Thirst

There have been many other times during which I felt a desperate thirst for water. My dad is a consultant forester, and sometimes I worked with him, marking timber all morning and afternoon; during the hot, humid summer days in the thorn-bush and nettle jungles of Indiana. I recall times feeling so thirsty I would have given nearly anything for a nice, cool glass of water.

Yet, with all the memories of being thirsty, I know there are people in the world who have thirsted for water with greater intensity than I have ever experienced. People have even died of thirst. I can't help but ponder the question—how much would they have given for a drink of water? Surely, they would have given all their possessions.

Let us consider this thought further, imagining ourselves having gone days without water in the desert. The sun is burning our skin. Our lips are cracked. Our mouths are so dry that our tongues feel like leather. We are growing faint. It is only a matter of time before we die from severe dehydration. Out of nowhere, we run across someone who says he knows where we can get water. He tells us there is a stream within five to ten miles of where we are. He also informs us that the path we must take to get to the stream is exceedingly dangerous. In fact, we could be killed making the journey. There promises to be deep crevices that we must cross, dreadfully high ledges so narrow we could easily slip to our deaths and poisonous plants with razor-sharp thorns reaching out to pierce our skin. We would face these dangers while suffering from extreme exhaustion incurred through climbing and trekking in the blistering dry heat of the desert, all the while nearly dying of thirst. Then we would be faced with a decision—do we continue walking on the flat sands, hoping we will run across some water soon, or do we hike in the dangerous direction where we know there is water? Either way is risky. Ultimately, regardless of the risk, our thirst will drive us to go in the direction of the dangerous hike. Why? Because we know there is water on the other side. We think to ourselves, *"What have I got to lose? If I continue in the direction I'm going, I will die if I don't find water soon. Which is really more risky—the treacherous hike to the stream or the hike of ease to no water? I am so thirsty for water that I will choose the hike toward the stream. If I die, I die. But at least I know I am going in the direction of water."* When we are thirsty enough for water, literally dying of thirst, we will risk losing everything for a drink of water.

Dying of Hunger

Hunger is similar to thirst. When someone is hungry for food, they have an intense craving. Food gives the body energy and the mind the ability to concentrate. It also gives a person the strength needed to function in everyday life. The human body can go a significantly long period without food, even longer than going without water. It will take the body more time to feel the extreme effects of hunger than the effects of thirst.

I cannot honestly say that I have been to the point of feeling so hungry that I thought I was going to die. The longest I have gone without food was during a fast the Lord led me into for seven days. Even though I was hungry at the end of my fast, I realized that those hunger pains were not nearly as severe as those of someone who has been malnourished for months or even years.

I have heard stories of people getting lost in the wilderness and being so hungry that when a person in their group died, they actually cooked and ate the dead person. This makes me think of an occasion written in the Old Testament about a severe famine in ancient Samaria:

> There was a great famine in the city; the siege lasted so long that a donkey's head sold for eighty shekels of silver, and a quart of a cab of seed pods for five shekels. As the king of Israel was passing by on the wall, a woman cried to him, "Help me, my lord the king!" The king replied, "If the LORD does not help you, where can I get help for you? From the threshing floor? From the winepress?" Then he asked her, "What's the matter?" She answered, "This woman said to me, 'Give up your son so we may eat him today, and tomorrow we'll eat my son.' So we cooked my son and ate him. The next day I said to her, 'Give up your son so we may eat him,' but she had hidden him" (2 Kings 6:25–29).

It is difficult to imagine being so hungry that we would consider murdering, cooking and eating our own children. That kind of hunger is more severe than most have ever experienced. When people are hungry enough for food, that craving will push them to take measures they may have once thought foolish and crazy. Most people, hopefully, would never stoop so low as to actually eat their own children. However, any person dying of hunger would risk their very life, if need be, to obtain food and satisfy hunger.

The One Desire of the Hungry and Thirsty

When someone is dying of hunger or thirst, life or death is not really the main concern. Death may even appear as a welcome relief, an end to that person's hunger or thirst. For someone dying of hunger, the ultimate desire is to have his or her hunger satisfied. Until that person's immense hunger is relieved, all he or she can think about is food and how gratifying it will be to eat again. For someone dying of thirst, the ultimate desire is to have his or her thirst quenched with water. Until that person's thirst is quenched, all he or she can think about is water and how refreshing it will be to drink it again.

Small Desires vs. Strong Desires

The words *hunger* and *thirst* instinctively make us think of a living creature's strong desire for water and food. But is there a more significant meaning behind the words *hunger* and *thirst*?[9]

> **Hunger**—discomfort caused by a need for food, starvation, a desire for food, any strong desire.[10]

> **Thirst**—the discomfort caused by a need for drink, a strong desire; craving.[11]

There are many things people hunger and thirst for in this world. A true hunger and thirst for something should not be confused with having a small desire. All of us have small desires. Small desires include things we enjoy, things we think need to be done, and things we would like to see happen. However, small desires do not completely consume our thoughts or attention; they are not worth taking extreme risks to accomplish.

In my own life, I have many small desires. One of these is gardening. My desire is strong enough to actually take the time to go out each spring, till the ground, and plant seeds. It is exciting to watch the plants grow. I care for my garden when I can, but honestly, if the plants in my garden do not appear to be healthy, I will not pour out all my energy to revive my garden. I enjoy working in it, but I'm not going to exhaust myself, spend a fortune or take great risks to have a good garden. Gardening is a small desire.

Each of us has varied small desires, such as things we enjoy doing and things we think need to be done. Some of these desires are greater or more important than others, but they still would not be considered the driving force behind our lives, nor would they determine how we live.

When we have a hunger and thirst for something, that focus determines how we spend our time. It consumes our thinking and dictates how we spend our money. It dominates our speech. It becomes the purpose for which we live. Some people hunger and thirst for money, fame or power. Some people hunger and thirst for a particular religion, cause or agenda. Some people hunger and thirst for their work, a hobby or a certain sport. Some people hunger and thirst for alcohol or drugs. Some people hunger and thirst for pleasure, comfort and a life of ease. Whatever the object of our desire, the gratification of this craving ultimately becomes the driving force of our lives.

Unfortunately, while this driving force varies from person to person, it is often not beneficial. Actually, many of the things people hunger and thirst for do more harm than good. Take for example a young woman who has a strong craving for heroine. She knows it may kill her if she continues using it, but still her body craves the drug. She is willing to risk death to satisfy her thirst for heroine. Or, consider a young man who has a strong craving to acquire more money. Becoming rich is his thirst and craving. Making more money is the driving force behind every decision he makes, and money consumes his every thought. He is willing to cheat, lie, belittle and even bring harm to other people, all in the name of making more money. He is willing to risk his reputation, integrity, family, other people and, if need be, even his own life to satisfy his hunger for worldly wealth.

To hunger and thirst for something differs from a small desire in that it consumes us and shapes the course of our lives through every decision we make. Unimaginable extremes are a small risk if we are able to pursue that thing for which we hunger and thirst. But how exactly do we pinpoint the one thing we are currently hungering and thirsting for more than anything else?

2

Our One Passion Revealed

"God will not accept a divided heart. He must be absolute monarch. There is not room in your heart for two thrones. Christ said: 'No man can serve two masters; for either he will hate the one and love the other, or else he will hold to the one and despise the other. Ye cannot serve God and Mammon.' Mark you, He did not say—'No man *shall* serve . . . Ye *shall* not serve . . . ', but 'No man *can* serve . . . Ye *can* not serve . . .' That means more than a command; it means that you cannot mix the worship of the true God with the worship of another god any more than you can mix oil and water. It cannot be done."[12]

- D.L. Moody

I t was my last year of college at Purdue University. One afternoon I was walking through campus to a particular park to pray. On my way there, I saw a young, beautiful lady I knew from a campus ministry we both attended. I was on the worship team for Campus Crusade for Christ (now known as CRU) and the lead singer of the worship team was the husband of this young lady's cousin. I had seen her a few times before but we never really talked except for cordial hellos to one another. However, I must admit, she always captured my attention when she was around.

On that particular day, I tried to think of some excuse to go talk to her. I remembered that on Friday evening I would be attending a fellowship gathering at someone's house. I knew she was probably going as well, and really wanted to ask her for a ride, but I also wanted to play it smooth. My plan was to ask her if her cousin and her cousin's husband were going to the fellowship gathering that Friday. If so, I'd ask her to inquire if her cousin would let me hitch a ride. This may seem silly, and you probably wonder why I didn't just ask her if she was going and could give me a ride, but when a guy likes a girl, sometimes he tries so hard to play it cool that he ends up acting like a fool. Honestly, I can't remember if I actually even needed a ride, but this was the only reason I could think of at the moment to go talk to her.

Nervously stepping toward her, I asked, *"Hey, how are you doing?"* We exchanged the usual awkward greetings. My mind and heart raced. I went on to ask her the question which I thought up to ask her, making it appear this was the reason I approached her. She told me her cousin was going, but what she said next made my heart feel as if it would literally jump out of my chest. She said to me, *"I'm going too, so you can just ride with me if you want."* My "plan" worked better than I thought. That was nearly ten years ago, and I am glad to say the young lady I approached that day is now my beautiful bride of nine years.

Sometimes the true desire of our heart is masked by good acting. On that day in college, I wanted to play it cool so the young lady would *think* I merely desired a ride to a house, when all the while, the true desire of my heart was to get to know her better. The revealing of my heart's desire in that situation is small in comparison to God revealing to us, at the end of our lives, the one desire and passion to which we have dedicated the entirety of our lives. At this moment, if God were to come to us and reveal our one, main desire and passion, what would be revealed?

Passion Defined

In the previous chapter, I discussed the meaning of truly hungering and thirsting for something. It means more than merely having a small desire. When we hunger and thirst for something, we have such a powerful desire for that thing that we naturally begin displaying certain characteristics in every area of our lives coinciding with our yearning. Our behavior, thinking and conversation begin to reflect our desire for that thing and this can now be defined as the one, central passion of our lives.

Many different Greek words can be translated into the word *passion* in the English Bible, but for the sake of this book, the English definition for the word *passion* will be the choice:

Passion—the object of any strong desire.[13]

The word *passion* is closely connected to the terms *hunger* and *thirst*. As stated earlier, both the terms *hunger* and *thirst* can be defined: a strong desire. Therefore, the word *passion* is the object for which we hunger and thirst. If we have a strong desire for food, food is our passion. If we have a strong desire for water, water is our passion.

Again . . . we must consider the overriding passion of our lives and genuinely meditate on this. Each of us must reflect upon understanding what the object of our strongest desire truly is. Before we shoot out an answer, we must do a thorough examination of every area of our lives. It is easy to say with our mouths what we believe or *want* to believe. However, our one main passion will be revealed as we measure and examine every single aspect of our lives.

Water Poured Out

Second Samuel 23 tells the account of when King David was besieged by the Philistines at a place called Adullam during the Philistine's occupation of Bethlehem. While there, David was extremely thirsty; Scripture actually says he *longed* for water. He was not just parched; he was desperately thirsty:

> David longed for water and said, "Oh, that someone would get me a drink of water from the well near the gate of Bethlehem!" So the three mighty men broke through the Philistine lines, drew water from the well near the gate of Bethlehem and carried it back to David. But he refused to drink it; instead, he poured it out before the LORD. "Far be it from me, O LORD, to do this!" he said. "Is it not the blood of men who went at the risk of their lives?" And David would not drink it (2 Samuel 23:13-17).

David's single, foremost passion was revealed. He was extremely thirsty for water and, at that moment, he thought the most important thing in the entire world was to relieve this thirst. After his men returned from their death-defying mission of fetching their king some water from Bethlehem, David had a choice to make. It was a time of testing. What would David do? Once David realized how his men risked their lives simply for the sake of water, he could not make himself drink it. Instead he immediately poured it out before the Lord saying, "Far be it from me, O LORD, to do this!" Why would

David do such a thing? Because at that moment, David realized it would honor God more to pour out the water before Him than to drink it. David knew this was what God wanted. Was David still thirsty for water? Of course! However, David revealed that his thirst for honoring and pleasing God was greater than his selfishness in relieving his thirst. The object of David's thirst, his one main passion, was revealed to be the Lord God.

Oh, how we need to come to the same place as David here in 2 Samuel! The place in our lives where we thirst for God more than anything else. The place where we can take our desire for money, power, pride, selfishness, sex, drugs, television, sports, hobbies, earthly treasures, religion, even our causes—and pour them out before the Lord crying out, *"Lord God, I long for you more than I do all of these things!"*

What could God do through our lives if we did such a thing? Each of us should ask ourselves—*"Is there anything in my life I desire more than God?"* David's fleshly thirst for water was competing with his thirst for God, and similarly we may have a thirst in our lives that is competing with our thirst for God. David chose to throw his water on the ground, showing his longing for God to be greater than his selfish longing for water. What will we choose to do? Whatever we decide will reveal the nature of our greatest passion, right now, in our lives.

3

Get This Right

"... you will find in Psalm 62:11: 'God hath spoken once; twice have I heard this; that POWER BELONGETH UNTO GOD.' I am glad it does. I am glad that power did not belong to D. L. Moody; I am glad that it did not belong to Charles G. Finney; I am glad that it did not belong to Martin Luther; I am glad that it did not belong to any other Christian man whom God has greatly used in this world's history. Power belongs to God."[14]

– R. A. Torrey

My wife is always getting on me for making up words that do not exist or using words in ways they were not meant to be used. (This gift is from my dad who also, unknowingly, makes up his own words.) Apparently growing up in the back-woods of southern Indiana didn't help build my vocabulary. However, I maintain that creating new words is a talent. It takes skill to think of a word not listed among the thousands of words in the English dictionary. Who says that just because a word doesn't appear in the English dictionary it is not really a word? Well, my wife for one. Along with this talent,

I also possess the "gift" of giving words definitions that do not belong to those specific words.

A couple of years ago I was amazed to discover that a statement I learned in high school did not actually mean what I thought it did. If you took driver's education in high school, you probably heard of the term *defensive driving*. Now, you may think me strange, but for some odd reason I always thought the term defensive driving meant that drivers were supposed to drive with confidence. They were not to be afraid while driving, but instead should be gutsy as they make quick and confident decisions to ensure their safety on the road. I remember thinking to myself that drivers who seemed unsure while driving, who made second guesses, and who were not confident in their driving ability needed a lesson in defensive driving. That is what I *used* to think.

A few years ago, I was talking with my wife about how people needed to be defensive drivers and explaining to her what I thought the term meant. After doing this, she looked at me like I was crazy and then laughed at me. She proceeded to tell me the true definition of the term defensive driving. Apparently, it refers to being aware of what other cars might do on the road, watching out for potential hazards and being on the defense. I was dumbfounded as I realized what I believed all those years—was wrong! Thankfully, now I know the true definition of the term defensive driving.

Significance of Meaning

The words we use express meaning. When we speak, write a letter, send an email or twitter a message the words we choose convey a meaning, both to us and to the person receiving them. Hopefully, the meaning of those words is the same thing to us as it is to the person to whom we are communicating.

If I tell someone in my house that our house is on fire, and I understand those words to literally mean that *our house is on fire*, but the person I am speaking to believes those words to mean that the *inside of our house is hot*, they might tell me to turn on the air-conditioner. However, if our house is literally on fire, an air-conditioner will not help. It is vital that the other person in the house understand the intended meaning of my words.

We as Christians can often do a similar thing with words and statements. We may read passages in the Bible or hear sermons preached but often fail to grasp their full and appropriate meaning. We may even say such things as—"*The Bible says we just need to believe in Jesus,*" or "*The Bible says we need to trust God,*" or "*The Bible says we need to have faith.*" But how often do we actually take the time to appreciate and take hold of the full Biblical meaning behind such truths? Too many of us are satisfied enough in our Christian walk with simply knowing the quick Sunday school answers to the Bible; answers we have read in a particular book or have heard someone else say.

Some of us may be familiar with just enough of the Bible to get us into trouble. I fear many of us Christians are convinced, at least in our own minds, that we rightly understand and apply the teachings of Scripture even though we do not regularly read and meditate upon them. If that be the case, we are in danger of unknowingly believing things about Scripture that are not true, incorrectly defining statements in the Bible and living out our lives in ways that are inconsistent with the teachings of God's Word. We can too easily be deceived into thinking we have a correct understanding of something scriptural, when in fact we do not. Satan is thrilled if we *think* we rightly understand, apply and live out a specific teaching in God's word when in reality we do not.

All of God's word requires tender care. As we read the Bible, we must meditate upon and pray over each word, concept and statement. Through this approach, we will come to a greater understanding of the teachings of the Bible. But, let us not confuse our understanding of those truths with actually applying those truths to our lives. The knowledge must translate into application in our personal lives.

In this way, the Lord has been continually impressing one specific verse upon my heart. It is found in the Beatitudes of Jesus: "Blessed are those who hunger and thirst for righteousness, for they will be filled" (Matthew 5:6). I am fully persuaded that God desires each of us to thoroughly comprehend the full meaning of this verse and appropriately live it out in our lives.

Jesus, Please Explain

In Matthew 15, Jesus is sharing a parable with the crowds who have come to hear Him. Once Jesus is finished speaking, Peter comes to Jesus saying, "Explain to us the parable" (Matthew 15:15). Jesus "did not say anything to [the crowds] without using a parable" (Mark 4:34a). To His disciples, however, Jesus reveals greater truth: "But when he was alone with his own disciples, He explained everything" (Mark 4:34b).

Peter, as one of Jesus' closest disciples, is able to come to Jesus and say, "Explain to us the parable." Likewise, before we continue to think about what it means to hunger and thirst after righteousness, it is vital we fall down on our knees, draw close to Jesus and ask Him to explain to us the true meaning of hungering and thirsting for righteousness. The words expressed in this book can only explain so much, but Jesus Christ can open our hearts so that we are able to grasp the fullness of what it means to hunger and thirst for righteousness.

We desperately need Jesus to open our eyes to the full meaning of His statement, "Blessed are those who hunger and thirst for righteousness, for they will be filled" (Matthew 5:6). Perhaps we too readily assume that we have the basic idea of these words and are satisfied with that understanding. It would be beneficial to ask ourselves a few questions: What if we are wrong about what we think Jesus means? How thoroughly have we studied, meditated and prayed over Matthew 5:6 to see if our understanding of this verse is correct? What if there is more to Jesus' meaning than we assume? What if our lack of understanding of these words is actually hindering us from seeing their fullness played out in our personal lives?

These are humbling questions to consider, but still we must. Let us not be too proud to contemplate the possibility that we may not fully grasp the meaning behind this verse in Matthew. James 4:6 says, "God opposes the proud but gives grace to the humble." Let us humble ourselves before the Lord and ask Him to give us a correct understanding of Matthew 5:6 and He will be graceful toward us and answer our prayer.

More than a Basic Understanding

I am convinced that very few Christians are experiencing the fullness of Matthew 5:6. This one little verse is jam-packed with grandeur and richness, and therefore we cannot afford to simply have a basic understanding of it. God has so much more He wants to reveal to us. We need only listen and allow Him to teach our hearts. God desires to move us far beyond a basic understanding of the words found in this verse to the point where we personally understand their reality in our lives.

Being satisfied with a rudimentary understanding of Matthew 5:6 is like a child who sees a painting of the ocean and then believes he grasps the basic magnificence of the ocean through that painting. He doesn't find it necessary to go see the ocean himself because he is satisfied enough with the painting. But, in no way does the painting express the full magnificence of the ocean. To be satisfied with the painting when the boy could experience the real thing is ludicrous. What great splendor this boy is missing out on!

Think of it another way. It is like a colorblind man who refuses to be cured of his colorblindness because he believes he understands color from other people's explanation. He *says* he is satisfied. However, in no way does the colorblind man comprehend the brilliance of color simply from what others have spoken about color. To be satisfied with a basic understanding of color, as explained and defined by someone else, when he could experience seeing the brilliance of color with his own eyes is absurd.

Personally, I do not want a basic understanding of Matthew 5:6. None of us should. Jesus says we are blessed if we hunger and thirst for righteousness, and we who do so will be filled. Let us not be satisfied to merely grasp the *gist* of what Jesus is saying. Let us yearn to grasp the *fullness* of what Jesus is saying. May our spirits ache to receive and experience the actual blessing and fulfillment of Jesus' promise.

Stay Close to Jesus

As already discussed, intellectually comprehending a certain truth is not the same thing as experiencing the fullness of that truth. Jesus must be the One who brings out the fullness of Matthew 5:6 to us. Being close to Jesus, as Peter was, is especially important when wanting a deeper understanding of His truth. The further away from Jesus we are, the less we will grasp the extensiveness of God's word.

The closer we are to Jesus, the deeper we will grasp God's word. It is essential that we study, read and gain a solid understanding of God's word, but unless we remain close to Jesus[15], we will never experience the fullness of God's word in our lives.

As we continue to unveil the truths of Matthew 5:6, let's divide this piece of Scripture into two sections. The first section of this verse, "Blessed are those who hunger and thirst for righteousness," is discussed in Chapters 4 and 5. The second section of this verse, "for they will be filled," is discussed in Chapter 6.

4

Hunger and Thirst
for Righteousness (Part I)

Part I

"No amount of money, genius, or culture can move things
for God. Holiness energizing the soul, the whole man aflame
with love, with desire for more faith, more prayer, more
zeal, more consecration—this is the secret of power."[16]

– E.M. Bounds

The Lord has blessed my wife and me with three lovely children. Leighton is six; Gabriel is four; and Elizabeth is two. These are *interesting* times for us, if you know what I mean. I find it hard to believe that just over six years ago, my wife and I were by ourselves in a quiet house. Now, our house is booming with activity, and quietness only comes as a dream. Nevertheless, I must say that I love my children immeasurably. While our house is chaotic at times, I fully believe the promise from Scripture regarding children: "Sons are a heritage from the LORD, children a reward from him" (Psalm

127:3). However, I must confess and repent of the moments when I seem to forget this promise in Scripture.

Children can be demanding; especially when it comes to food. My wife and I are tested daily in the area of patience. Our two oldest children, Leighton and Gabriel, have a common phrase they repeat nearly a hundred or more times a day—*"I'm hungry!"* From the time they get up in the morning until they go to bed at night, we hear the refrain—*"I'm hungry!"* Often times, after our boys have been griping about being hungry, my wife will set a good homemade meal before them. They will take one or two bites and then stop eating. We urge them to eat their meal, but instead of eating, they will say, *"I'm all done,"* or *"I don't want to eat."* Then, just a few minutes after the meal they refused to eat, that familiar phrase pops out of their mouths again, *"I'm still hungry!"* Sometimes, as parents, we feel like throwing our hands up in the air and screaming.

For good reasons, I am perplexed. My boys repeatedly cry out that they are hungry, but when they don't eat the meals placed before them, I question their hunger. For what do my children hunger? At these moments, I question if my children even know what they truly want. They know they want something, so they say, *"I'm hungry,"* but they don't quite understand how to satisfy their hunger. Similarly, so many people sense, within the depths of their spirit, a hunger and thirst for *something more* in their life, but how many comprehend the way to truly satisfy that longing?

Not Satisfied

We live in a world of discontentment. Every human being has a longing to be filled or satisfied with something. But the question is—with what are we trying to satisfy ourselves?

Each of us should take some time to dwell upon our lives and ask ourselves some honest questions: *"Do I feel fully satisfied? Do I feel as if something is missing?"* We may not be able to put our finger on it, but many of us just feel like there *has* to be something more to life than what we are currently experiencing. Some of us may have tried to find satisfaction by climbing the corporate ladder of success. Some of us may have tried to find satisfaction in the building of our own kingdoms—gaining property, building a nice house, having a decent car or truck and making sure there is always enough money in our bank account. Some of us may have tried to find satisfaction in other people, even our own families. Some of us may have tried to find satisfaction in religion—by going to church, doing religious activities, following religious traditions and associating ourselves with religious people. If any of this describes what we are living for, we will never be completely satisfied and will always sense a longing for more. Perhaps some of us have already arrived at that place where these things aren't as fulfilling as they once were, and now, we want more.

Sometimes we think the best way to quiet our longing is by staying busy with all sorts of different activities. I have even heard it said the way to keep our youth out of trouble is to keep them busy in sports, church and extra-curricular activities. However, busyness is not the answer. There are many youth trying to find fulfillment by getting involved in all types of programs, even church activities. Yet, at the end of the day, they still feel empty. While being involved can be a good thing, it is not the answer to our youth's troubles. Even young people have a desperate longing in their hearts which they are seeking to fulfill.

Each and every one of us has a longing within our hearts for something more. Busying ourselves with sports, events, jobs, volunteer work, social clubs, family gatherings and church activities is not the answer to finding ultimate satisfaction. It can be good to be involved, grow socially and work hard, but too often our constant busyness only hides the ultimate dissatisfaction of our hearts. It would be beneficial for each of us to stop busying ourselves for a while; evaluate that with which we are trying to satisfy our lives; and begin heeding to the words: "Be still, and know that I am God" (Psalm 46:10).

Story of My Life

Right before I graduated from high school, I had a sense of discontentment in my own life. In high school my desire was to be popular, please everyone and be a decent kid. I was on the sports teams. I had lots of friends. I had a girlfriend. I had a loving family. I was healthy. I went to church. I was baptized when I was ten. I considered myself a good person. Things were going well in my life. My desires were being fulfilled. But starting my senior year, I began to sense a growing dissatisfaction in my life. This became a constant struggle for me. I sincerely dwelt upon the fact that, even though I considered myself a Christian, I was not fully surrendering everything in my life to the Lord.

The summer after I graduated high school, I went to a Billy Graham Crusade in Indianapolis, Indiana. It was there that God powerfully spoke to me. At the end of the program hundreds of people made their way forward as the song "Just as I Am" played in the background. In that moment, I heard God speak loudly within my heart, *"Adam, you have a choice. You can continue living as you are and go down a path of continual struggle and frustration, or you can surrender your all to Me and begin to experience all I can do through a surrendered individual."* Needless to say, I began weeping, went forward and turned my entire life over to God. That night, in the summer of 1999, began my journey of discovering the source of true, lasting and absolute satisfaction.

After my encounter with God, I spent many nights crying out to God. I was not satisfied with simply going through the motions of life. Within the depths of my being there was a hunger and thirst for God. I wanted more of Him and longed to know Him and please Him with my life. I did not instantaneously become a solid, mature Christian. I had many struggles and issues that God began working out of me. Even today, while I may be much more mature in my faith than when I was eighteen, I still am not even close to full maturity. Just ask my wife! However, God broke me that day at the Billy Graham Crusade and began redirecting my heart's hunger and thirst. Since then, God has gradually been directing me towards His ultimate source of lasting satisfaction in life.

Unveiling Righteousness

Jesus says, "Blessed are those who hunger and thirst for righteousness, for they will be filled" (Matthew 5:6). We must not overlook the profoundness of this verse—Jesus is telling us how to be completely filled in our lives. Hungering and thirsting for righteousness is what will bring true satisfaction to us. Some might be thinking, "*Um, okay, that's good and all, but what does it mean to hunger and thirst for righteousness?*" That's a good question. But before answering that question, we must first understand the meaning of—righteousness.

May the following ten insights into the concept of righteousness open each of our minds to the significance of righteousness. I pray this small taste will ignite in us a yearning to achieve a greater understanding of righteousness in our own, personal lives.

5

Hunger and Thirst
for Righteousness (Part II)

Part II

"Where we read in Scripture of the desires, longings, and thirstings of the saints, righteousness and God's laws are much more frequently mentioned as the object of them, than anything else."[17]

- Jonathan Edwards

Insight #1: Righteousness and Believing the Lord God

If you are like me, you probably hear the term *believe* thrown around all the time. Politicians tell us to believe their message. Our parents may have told us more than once, *"Believe me, because I'm your parent, I'm older, and I know better!"* Many religious people of all faiths tell us, *"You must believe and have faith."* It seems everyone everywhere is telling us to believe them, have faith in them and trust them. Perhaps we have been lied to so many times that we don't know who or what to believe anymore.

In a world full of lies, crooked philosophies and deception, there is One in whom we can fully believe, One who always speaks the truth and is always faithful to His word. Towards the end of King David's prayer in 2 Samuel 27:28, David prays, "O Sovereign LORD, you are God! Your words are trustworthy." Scripture also tells us, "Know therefore that the LORD your God is God; he is the faithful God, keeping his covenant of love to a thousand generations of those who love him and keep his commands" (Deuteronomy 7:9). The Lord God is completely faithful, and His word is always true.

It is the Lord God alone who is faithful and true; the God who is Jehovah (YHWH); the God of Scripture; the God of Abraham, Isaac and Jacob; the God who sent His Son Jesus Christ into the world to bring salvation to those who believe; the God who raised Jesus from the grave; the God who is Father, Son and Holy Spirit; the God who has revealed Himself through Scripture. The Lord God must not be confused with any other god of any other religion. King David writes about the Lord God, "There is no one like You, O LORD, and there is *no God but you*, as we have heard with our own ears" (1 Chronicles 17:20, emphasis mine). The psalmist also makes it clear, "Let them know that you, whose name is the LORD—that *you alone* are the Most High over all the earth" (Psalm 83:18, emphasis mine).

In Genesis 15:1-5, the Lord comes to Abraham and says He will bless Abraham with a son and many offspring. Then right after the Lord speaks this promise to Abraham, verse 6 says Abraham "believed the LORD, and he credited to him as righteousness." Don't miss the significance of this verse. Abraham simply believed, and the Lord equated that belief as righteousness.

The act of believing God and the condition of righteousness are inseparable. Abraham believed God, and God credited that belief as righteousness. Therefore, to truly hunger and thirst for righteousness, we must first seek to come to a place in our lives where we fully believe every word spoken by God.

Friends, we must stop doubting God's word. The book of James tells us, ". . . he who doubts is like a wave of the sea, blown and tossed by the wind. That man should not think he will receive anything from the Lord" (James 1:6b-7). God is faithful and true in all He says. Therefore, we must believe everything He says and continually align our beliefs, decisions and actions with His word. Belief and action go hand in hand.

When we believe God, He credits that belief as righteousness to us. When we do not believe Him, it is not righteousness which will be credited to us, rather the very opposite—unrighteousness or wickedness. If ever we doubt God, we should fall to our knees, repent of this act of unrighteousness, and cry out alongside the man in the gospel of Mark, "I do believe; help me overcome my unbelief!" (Mark 9:24). He who is Faithful and True will hear our prayer and answer.

Insight #2: Righteousness and Justice

Recently, I was watching the afternoon news on television and there was a story about a murder. During an interview, the mother of the young man who had been murdered declared that she would not be satisfied until the man who murdered her son was put to death. She mentioned how much better she would sleep at night when she knew justice had been done. This mother was deeply hurt. Her son had been taken from her. Her pain was great. While it bothered me somewhat that this broken-hearted mother longed for the death of this man and seemed exceptionally unforgiving, seeing this woman's reaction made me stop and reflect on a reality. In the heart of every human being there is a longing for justice to be done.

Throughout Scripture, righteousness and justice are often mentioned together. God speaks in the book of Isaiah, "Maintain justice and do what is right, for my salvation is close at hand and my righteousness will soon be revealed" (Isaiah 56:1). The psalmist says of the Lord, "Clouds and thick darkness surround him; righteousness and justice are the foundation of his throne" (Psalm 97:2). Since righteousness and justice are the foundation of God's throne, we must assume that they are extremely important to Him, and therefore important to us, as believers, as well.

Righteousness, in the simplest sense, means "that which is right, true and just." Justice has to do with fairness—doing what is right, true and deserved. The woman whose son was murdered rightly understood the unjustness of the crime committed. Her desire was for the murderer to be rightly punished for his wrongdoing. In other words, she understood her son's murder was not the right thing to do (*righteousness*) and therefore a price needed to be paid (*justice*).

Justice and righteousness cannot be separated. A few questions may arise at this point: Who defines what is right? When the right thing is determined, who is ultimately the one who makes certain that true justice is done? The answer to these two questions is—God does. For Scripture says about God, "righteousness and justice are the foundation of his throne" (Psalm 97:2).

As already stated, every person has within them a desire for justice to be done. However, this desire must not be separated from true righteousness which comes from God. When we desire justice to be done apart from God's righteousness, we run the risk of taking matters in our own hands and causing more injustice. We live in a depraved and fallen world. Violence, corruption, greed, selfishness and wickedness run rampant as a result of sin entering the world. Babies are being murdered. Girls are being forced to become sex objects. Husbands are beating their wives. Millions are being killed through genocide. Thousands are dying from starvation. And much of this arises out of the selfishness of others. Even a close look within ourselves reveals corruption, deeds born from selfish motives, hurtful words rashly spoken and an abundance of impure thoughts. If we think long and hard about the sinful condition of our world, and even of ourselves, it is sickening.

A price must be paid for all the corruption and injustice. Thanks be to God a price has been paid. God sent His one and only Son, Jesus Christ, into the world to die on a cross. Jesus' blood was the payment for sin. Jesus' blood is the cost of salvation. Only through Jesus' blood is there purification and forgiveness. In Jesus' death, justice has been met in regard to sin. However, everything is yet to be finalized. The sacrifice has been made for the forgiveness of sin, but the judgment of all sin is yet to come. Three days after Jesus died, God raised Him to life. Soon afterwards Jesus ascended. And God's word promises that Jesus will return one day. When Jesus comes the second time, He is coming in glory; and in His righteousness, He will destroy sin once and for all.

If we are still in our sins when we die or when Jesus comes again, justice will be done for our sin. If our sins have never been removed from us, we will be punished for our sins and face the wrath of a holy, just and righteous God. We are in desperate need of Jesus' blood for the forgiveness of sin. As previously said, in Jesus' death, justice has been met in regards to sin. If we are not in Christ and Christ in us, justice has not yet been done in regards to our sin. Without Jesus we are considered unrighteous.[18] We must repent of our sins and believe in Him.

Though we still struggle with our sinful flesh and the corruption of the world around us, for those of us who believe upon Jesus Christ, our sins have already been dealt with because we have been washed clean by His blood. The psalmist reminds us about God, "You love righteousness and hate wickedness" (Psalm 45:7). We who are believers must also love righteousness and abhor wickedness, which will make us long for God's justice to be completed. Hungering and thirsting for righteousness means we long for wickedness to be done away with in our own lives, and we now show the truth of that longing through the purity of our lives. Also, hungering and thirsting for righteousness means we desire justice to be done by God for all the wickedness which has already happened, all the wickedness still happening, and all the wickedness yet to happen in this world.

Since righteousness and justice always go hand in hand, hungering and thirsting for righteousness means believers should have within their souls a deep longing for the corruption of this world to be dealt with and to see an end to the war temptations wage against their own sinful flesh. In Revelation 6, those who have been martyred because of their faith in Jesus Christ cry out to God, "How long, Sovereign Lord, holy and true, until you judge the inhabitants of the earth and avenge our blood!" (Revelation 6:10). Similarly, each believer should have an intense longing for God's justice to be done, and for all things to be made right. In turn, this longing will cause, within the believer's heart, an immense yearning for the coming of Jesus Christ as Judge.

Insight #3: Righteousness and the Word of God

My younger brother is working with my dad, a consulting forester in Indiana. The objective is for my brother to eventually take over and operate the business. It would be absurd to think that my brother is simply going to take over the business without first being trained in forestry and business. First, he had to spend four years in college studying forestry. After graduation, he started working with my dad and gradually began learning how to operate the business for himself. He is now approaching the point where he could take over the business and my dad could retire. It has taken much schooling, studying and training for my brother to stand where he is today. Without that training, he could not have done it.

Before someone becomes a doctor, they must first study and train. Before an athlete becomes a professional athlete, they dedicate many years to practice and training. Before any of us can fully understand anything, we must first study, learn and train. Why would it be any different when it comes to learning how to live in righteousness?

Righteousness does not come naturally for us. The book of Ecclesiastes says, "There is not a righteous man on earth who does what is right and never sins" (Ecclesiastes 7:20). Ever since sin has entered the world, all humanity has become unrighteous. Righteousness is unnatural to our sinful flesh. Therefore, we must understand what it is to be righteous, and we must train ourselves in righteousness. How do we do this?

The apostle Paul writes, "All Scripture is God-breathed and is useful for teaching, rebuking, correcting and training in righteousness" (2 Timothy 3:16). Scripture trains us how to live in righteousness. Consequently, if we do not know and understand Scripture, we will not know and understand righteousness.

How much does the average Christian read, study and meditate on Scripture? I fear too many Christians, particularly here in the United States, are lethargic when it comes to understanding Scripture. I cannot help but wonder how many Bibles are taken to a church gathering on Sunday and then left in the car until the next Sunday. For that matter, how many people actually bring their Bible to a church gathering anymore? Sadly in our day, we have many deacons, elders and workers in the church, regardless of how many years they may have been attending church, with as much knowledge of Scripture as many of the youth in Sunday school. We also have an alarming number of youth in the church learning Bible stories and moral lessons who think that the gist of Christianity is simply about believing in God's existence, going to church, being nice and saying prayers when trouble comes.

It is troubling when I try having a deep conversation with a Christian—about a Scripture passage, or God in general—and it quickly becomes obvious that the person finds the conversation boring, uncomfortable or treats it like a foreign subject. Honestly, it is becoming the exception to find Christians who know enough about Scripture to talk about it; or who actually show real excitement and joy over talking about Scripture. The truth of these types of scenarios among confessing Christians is troubling indeed.

Scripture is becoming more and more foreign to the hearts, minds and everyday lives of the church in the United States. Where are the men and women who take delight in the Scripture like the psalmist who wrote, "Oh, how I love your law! I meditate on it all day long" (Psalm 119:97)? Television, games, sports, movies and simple busyness keep people so occupied that many are finding it hard to take the time to meditate on Scripture anymore. In the midst of all the myriad of distractions, is it really any wonder why so many Christians seem to be losing their passion for Scripture and the things of God?

The apostle Paul writes, "Anyone who lives on milk, being still an infant, is not acquainted with the teaching about righteousness. But solid food is for the mature, who by constant use have trained themselves to distinguish good from evil" (Hebrews 5:13-14). We are in dire need of training in the way of righteousness. If we are not trained, we are considered infants in God's eyes. Infants are limited in their abilities. A Christian infant will be hindered in his or her effectiveness for God's Kingdom.

Those who are mature in their faith understand the vital need for God's word as the way to comprehend righteousness and live righteously. They acquire a genuine love for reading and meditating upon Scripture, find joy in discussing and studying Scripture with other believers, and desire to hear the preaching or teaching of Scripture as often as possible. Truly hungering and thirsting for righteousness means having a deep longing to understand and know the depths of Scripture. Scripture trains and instructs in the way of righteousness. The hungry and thirsty pour themselves into Scripture every chance they get.

Insight #4: Righteousness and God's Character

Who do you want to be like when you grow up? How many times have we heard a little child respond to this question with a big grin saying, "*I want to be just like my dad when I grow up*"? Depending on the character of the child's dad, that aspiration may or may not be a good thing.

But we have a perfect example in our Heavenly Father. Scripture reveals our ideal Dad. The Heavenly Father is Father to all who put their faith in Jesus Christ. He is a Father who is perfectly good and one who loves and takes delight in His children. When we are born again we become a new creature in Christ Jesus and are given the Holy Spirit. The Holy Spirit within us "testifies with our spirit that we are God's children" (Romans 8:16). How gloriously fulfilling it is to know that we who have been washed clean by the blood of Jesus Christ are now children of God!

With this in mind, it would be beneficial for each of us to ask ourselves, "*Who do I want to be like when I grow up?*" That might sound like a strange question for some of us, but from the perspective of eternity, it really isn't odd at all. The Heavenly Father is characterized by holiness, goodness, kindness, mercy, love, justness, grace and so much more. Therefore, every believer should enthusiastically be able to say, "*I want to be just like my Heavenly Father!*" The apostle Paul shared in this enthusiasm when he wrote, "Be imitators of God, therefore, as dearly loved children" (Ephesians 5:1). God's desire for each of us is to be just like Him. Only through the power of the Holy Spirit can we become increasingly like our Heavenly Father. We are called to imitate the character of God.

So, how is it possible for us to be such imitators of God? First, we must understand the character of God. If I were asked to sum up God's character in one word, I would choose—RIGHTEOUSNESS. Righteousness is so deeply embedded into God's character that all of His actions and decrees come about because of His righteousness. The psalmist writes, "Your righteousness reaches to the skies, O God, you who have done great things. Who, O God, is like you?" (Psalm 71:19). In the book of Isaiah, God says, "But my righteousness will last forever, my salvation through all generations" (Isaiah 51:8). Isaiah also describes God as one who speaks in righteousness.[19] Furthermore, it is written in Isaiah, "But the LORD Almighty will be exalted by his justice, and the holy God will show himself holy by his righteousness" (Isaiah 5:16). God is righteous and is therefore completely holy, entirely true, always right, perfectly just and flawlessly good.

The apostle Paul writes to the church in Ephesus,

> You were taught, with regard to your former way of life, to put off your old self, which is being corrupted by its deceitful desires; to be made new in the attitude of your

minds; and to put on the new self, created to be like God
in true righteousness and holiness (Ephesians 4:22-24).

God's goal for us as His people is to become like Him in
righteousness and holiness. Yet, we cannot do it on our own. God is
the One who must do this work through us. The book of Jeremiah
speaks about God, "This is the name by which he will be called: The
LORD Our Righteousness" (Jeremiah 23:6). The Lord God is our
righteousness. We can only become righteous through Him. And
God has made it possible for us to share in His righteousness through
Jesus Christ's death and resurrection.

Hungering and thirsting for righteousness means we deeply desire
to be like God; craving to be ones who are holy, true and perfect
just like Him while understanding that we cannot achieve our own
righteousness apart from God, because He alone is our righteousness.
As God's children, our yearning to be like Him ought to continually
motivate us to go to His word to learn about Him. Let us be ones
who cry out to God through prayer, *"Father God, I want to be just like
You. I know I cannot do it on my own. Fill me with Your Spirit. Empower
me to be righteous as You are righteous and to live in righteousness every
single second of every day."*

Insight #5: Righteousness and Christ Jesus

As Christians, we must understand that Jesus Christ is central to
what we believe. Without the death and resurrection of Jesus Christ,
we have nothing at all. Why? Because Jesus is the promised Messiah,
the One the prophets in the Old Testament prophesied would come.
Jesus is the Son of God who came into the world with no sin and
lived a life upon this earth entirely free of sin. He is the Lamb of God
who, as He was crucified upon the cross, took upon Himself the sins

of the world. He is the One who died, was raised to life on the third day, and who is now at God the Father's right hand. The gospel of John reveals Jesus to be the Word of God made flesh (John 1:14), and goes even further by writing, "the Word was God" (John 1:1). The gospel of Matthew says Jesus is called Immanuel, which means: "God with us" (Matthew 1:23). Jesus is the promised Messiah, and amazingly enough, He truly is God with us.

Jesus Christ fulfilled the entirety of the law of God, meaning that never once did He do or think anything which was not in accordance with God's ordinances. For this reason, Jesus was and is the perfect sacrifice, the flawless Lamb of God. Only Jesus could take our sin from us. He is the only One worthy enough to wash us clean of our unrighteousness and the only One able to impart true righteousness to us. Jesus' sacrifice did not just remove our sin from us, but through His death and resurrection, His righteousness is actually given to us who believe in Him. The prophet Jeremiah boldly writes,

> "The days are coming," declares the LORD, "when I will raise up to David a righteous Branch, a King who will reign wisely and do what is just and right in the land. In his days Judah will be saved and Israel will live in safety. This is the name by which he will be called: The LORD Our Righteousness" (Jeremiah 23:5-6).

We know the Lord God is our righteousness, but to better understand what that means, we must look to Jesus Christ. In the book of 1 John, Jesus Christ is called "the Righteous One" (1 John 2:1). The prophet Isaiah declares, "From the ends of the earth we hear singing: 'Glory to the Righteous One'" (Isaiah 24:16). In addition, look at what the apostle Paul writes about the righteousness of God in his letter to the Romans:

But now a righteousness from God, apart from law, has been made known, to which the Law and the Prophets testify. This righteousness from God comes through faith in Jesus Christ to all who believe. There is no difference, for all have sinned and fall short of the glory of God, and are justified freely by his grace through the redemption that came by Christ Jesus. God presented him as a sacrifice of atonement, through faith in his blood. He did this to demonstrate his justice, because in his forbearance he had left the sins committed beforehand unpunished—he did it to demonstrate his justice at the present time, so as to be just and the one who justifies those who have faith in Jesus (Romans 3:21-26).

We must look to Jesus Christ, who is "the image of the invisible God" to see God's complete righteousness revealed. In some sense, we could say that Jesus Christ is God's Righteousness. The apostle Paul writes, "Christ is the end of the law so that there may be righteousness for everyone who believes" (Romans 10:4).

Ultimately, it could be said that hungering and thirsting for righteousness comes down to one thing—desiring Jesus Christ above everything else. As believers, Jesus Christ must be everything to us. We are not just to know about Him; we are to actually know Him and be known by Him. We are to live in relationship with Him every moment of our lives and learn how to be like Him. Jesus, the Righteous One, says, "I am the bread of life. He who comes to Me will never go hungry, and he who believes in me will never be thirsty" (John 6:35).

God greatly desires us to come to a place in our lives where our yearning for Jesus Christ outweighs our want for any other thing in our lives. In Jesus there is true life and eternal satisfaction. As believers, our heart cry ought to be as the apostle Paul's, "I want to know Christ and the power of His resurrection and the fellowship of sharing in His sufferings, becoming like him in his death and so, somehow, to attain to the resurrection from the dead" (Philippians 3:10-11). Does this truly describe the cry of our own hearts?

Insight #6: Righteousness and Believers

Exactly who do we become once we are born again? Scripture tells us we are saints, ambassadors of Christ, a holy priesthood, children of God, servants of God, strangers to this world, pilgrims and citizens of Heaven. In 2 Corinthians 5:21, we who are in Christ are called something that ought to render us speechless—"the righteousness of God." Isn't that amazing? We, as believers in Jesus Christ are considered "the righteousness of God." The very statement almost seems heretical. But it is not heresy; it is the truth of God.

Jesus says to us, "Be perfect, therefore, as your heavenly Father is perfect" (Matthew 5:48). Most of us might respond to this verse by saying, *"That is impossible. I cannot be perfect because I have already sinned. No one is perfect except God. If anyone says they are perfect, they are lying."* It is true that all have sinned, "for all have sinned and fallen short of the glory of God" (Romans 3:23). However, we must realize that in Christ Jesus we are new creatures. Once we repent of our sins, believe in Jesus Christ and confess Him as Lord, something happens to us. We become born again. We become a new creature.

The apostle Paul discusses what happened to our sin at the crucifixion of Jesus Christ: "For we know that our old self was crucified with him so that the body of sin might be done away with, that we should no longer be slaves to sin—because anyone who has died has been freed from sin" (Romans 6:6). Psalm 103:12 further states, "As far as the east is from the west, so far has he removed our transgressions from us." For us who are believers, God has completely removed our sin from us. We tend to sufficiently understand the aspect of Jesus dying for our sins. However, Jesus' death and resurrection did not just remove our sin from us. Something even greater happened.

Let us take a look again at 2 Corinthians 5:21 and stand amazed and humbled as we view the entire verse: "God made [Jesus] who had no sin to be sin for us, so that in him we might become the righteousness of God." Jesus Christ, being the perfect sacrifice as the Lamb of God, took upon Himself the sins of the world. Jesus, through His death on the cross, actually became our sin for us. This part is generally received by Christians as truth with thanksgiving. But let us not miss the second part of 2 Corinthians 5:21. Yes, Jesus took our sin, but in return we as believers received Jesus' righteousness. Our sin is credited to Christ, and Christ's righteousness is credited to us. Therefore, for those of us who are in Christ, God no longer sees us as sinners. Instead, He sees us as completely and wholly righteous—perfect as He is perfect. That is especially humbling because we did nothing at all to earn Jesus' righteousness. In the book of Romans we read, "But now a righteousness from God, apart from the law, has been made known, to which the Law and the Prophets testify. This righteousness from God comes through faith in Jesus Christ to all who believe" (Romans 3:21-22). What a marvelous and gracious truth that we as believers, through Jesus Christ, are considered the righteousness of God.

Hungering and thirsting for righteousness, therefore, also includes desiring the righteous, meaning—*true believers*. This means we will have a longing for people to become believers that they may be righteous, too. Our hearts ought to ache for the lost to be brought into God's Kingdom as we cry out in prayer for them. Do our hearts ache for the lost? Do we weep before God over specific individuals to be brought into His Kingdom?

It also means we will have an immense love for those who are already believers. Our love ought to be so passionate for the body of Christ that we yearn to be in fellowship with other believers—to worship with them, talk with them, pray with them, study God's word with them and constantly be a part of their lives. Too often people say they don't need to "go to church" or be around other Christians because they can be with God and talk with Him anywhere at anytime. It is true that we can be with God and talk with Him at any time in our lives, but that does not excuse us from being in fellowship with other believers. If we do not desire to be around other believers in fellowship, we need to check our hearts. Hebrews 10:25 says, "Let us not give up meeting together, as some are in the habit of doing, but let us encourage one another—and all the more as you see the Day approaching."

Our love for the body of Christ must be so strong that we yearn to be in fellowship with one another. It should cultivate within us a great desire to lift the church up in continual prayer and to nurture a longing for holiness, faith, purity, power and passion to fill the hearts of all believers through the Holy Spirit. How deep is our love for those who belong to the church?

Insight #7: Righteousness and the Holy Spirit

Shortly before His death, Jesus told His disciples, "But I tell you the truth: It is for your good that I am going away. Unless I go away, the Counselor will not come to you; but if I go, I will send him to you" (John 16:7). The Counselor to whom Jesus is referring is the Holy Spirit.

After Jesus' resurrection from the dead, He stayed on earth for a short while before He ascended into Heaven. Right before His ascension, He promised His disciples, ". . . you will receive power when the Holy Spirit comes upon you; and you will be my witnesses in Jerusalem, and in all Judea and Samaria, and to the ends of the earth" (Acts 1:8). Just a few days later, Jesus' promise was fulfilled as the Holy Spirit came upon the believers at Pentecost.

We who are born again are new creatures in Christ, and we now have the Holy Spirit of God living in us. Amazingly, Scripture tells us, "Don't you know that you yourselves are God's temple and that God's Spirit lives in you?" (1 Corinthians 3:16). God dwells in us as believers through the Holy Spirit. We are His temple. Anyone who has been born again has the Holy Spirit of God living in them, or they are not truly born again. The last part of Romans 8:9 explains, "And if anyone does not have the Spirit of Christ, he does not belong to Christ."

So, what does the Holy Spirit have to do with righteousness? Jesus answers this question when He speaks of the Holy Spirit,

> When he comes, he will convict the world of guilt in regard to sin and righteousness and judgment: in regard to sin, because men do not believe in me; in regard to righteousness, because I am going to the Father, where you can see me no longer; in regard to judgment, because the prince of this world now stands condemned (John 16:8-10).

In this passage, Jesus revealed that the Holy Spirit comes upon us and convicts us of our sin, opening our eyes to see and understand that we are not righteous and are in desperate need for a Savior. The Holy Spirit then draws us to understand our need for our sins to be washed clean through Jesus' blood. Secondly, the Holy Spirit convicts us of righteousness because we, in and of ourselves, do not know how to be righteous. Our hands, feet, minds and hearts are tainted with sin. God, therefore, places His Holy Spirit into us, showing us how to live righteously and then actually empowering us to live righteously. The apostle Paul writes, "But if Christ is in you, your body is dead because of sin, yet your spirit is alive because of righteousness" (Romans 8:10). Jesus Christ's righteousness is in us who believe and the Holy Spirit brings to us conviction to live in His righteousness. Gratefully, the Holy Spirit does even more than just convict us of our unrighteousness. He is also the power we need to actually live in righteousness. Thirdly, the Holy Spirit convicts us of judgment, giving us full understanding that the enemy has already been defeated by God. In the end, God's Kingdom will come because God has already won the battle through Jesus Christ. Therefore, the Holy Spirit will convict us not to live by our sinful nature any longer, because it has already been defeated. The Holy Spirit living in us opens our eyes to what it means to live in victory through His power. Scripture says that God has "set his seal of ownership on us, and put his Spirit in our hearts as a deposit, guaranteeing what is to come" (2 Corinthians 1:22).

Although we who have been born again have the Holy Spirit living in us, teaching us and empowering us to live in righteousness, stubbornly we still choose to give in to sin at times. Though each believer has the Holy Spirit living in him or her, not all believers are living full of the Holy Spirit. The Bible points out that we as believers have a choice either to walk in the Spirit or to walk according to our sinful nature:

> So I say, live by the Spirit, and you will not gratify the desires of the sinful nature. For the sinful nature desires what is contrary to the Spirit, and the Spirit what is contrary to the sinful nature. They are in conflict with each other,

so that you do not do what you want. But if you are led by
the Spirit, you are not under the law (Galatians 5:16-18).

We have the power in us, as believers, to live completely in
righteousness. So why do we, all too often, choose to live according
to our sinful nature?

Hungering and thirsting for righteousness means we must crave
the fullness of the Holy Spirit in our lives. Each of us as believers
ought to have such a strong desire to live in righteousness that we
desperately and continuously cry out to God, *"Fill me with Your Holy
Spirit, O God! I trust that Your Spirit already lives within me, but I repent
from gratifying the desires of my sinful nature too often. Empower me to live
by the Spirit that I may live righteously and not attempt to satisfy the desires
of my sinful nature. Let me know and experience the fullness of Your Spirit
and choose to live in this fullness on a daily basis. Amen."*

Insight #8: Righteousness and Fruit

How can we know if a fruit tree is healthy or not? By looking
to see if it bears good fruit or bad fruit. If it always produces bad
fruit, we know something is wrong with that tree. Too often when a
confessing Christian is confronted by someone else for not behaving
like a Christian, he or she responds by saying, *"You can't judge me,
because only God knows my heart."* Should we have to drill a hole into
the middle of a fruit tree to see whether or not its heart is good? No!
Just look at the tree's fruit.

God, indeed, knows our heart, but that truth does not excuse
our unrighteous behavior. Rather, it should make us tremble because
our unrighteous behavior reveals that something is wrong with
our hearts. If we as Christians repeatedly fail to display the fruit of

righteousness in our lives, we need to begin examining the purity of our hearts.

What is the fruit of righteousness? Much of what I am discussing in this chapter describes the fruit of righteousness—believing God, loving justice, loving God's word, loving Jesus Christ, loving believers, loving the Holy Spirit, living in purity and holiness. As we bear the fruits of righteousness, we are becoming more and more like Jesus Christ in the way we behave, think and speak.

With that being said, Scripture purposely describes the fruit of righteousness in one word—PEACE. Isaiah 32:17 says, "The fruit of righteousness will be peace; the effect of righteousness will be quietness and confidence forever." Righteousness and peace are inseparable. "Love and faithfulness meet together; righteousness and peace kiss each other" (Psalm 85:10). Where there is righteousness, there is always peace. Where there is peace, there is always righteousness. Therefore, believers, who are the righteousness of God, have a peace and confidence about them because of what Jesus Christ has done. They do not worry over things. They do not need to prove anything about themselves through their own works apart from Christ. Their lives are characterized by peace and assurance because their sole trust is in Jesus. The righteous understand that they simply need to abide in Christ alone. Period. They are not anxious about anything because they are constantly seeking after the righteousness of God as Jesus says, "But seek first [God's] kingdom and his righteousness, and all these things will be given to you as well" (Matthew 6:33).

The fruit of righteousness can therefore be summed up as a complete peace coming only from God through Jesus Christ our Lord. Those who bear the fruit of righteousness will show it in their lives by a quiet humility and a rock solid confidence in God in every aspect of their lives, as pointed out in Isaiah 32:17. Therefore, hungering and thirsting for righteousness means that all believers will desire to bear the fruit of righteousness in their lives—the complete "peace of God, which transcends all understanding" (Philippians 4:7). Rest assured, it won't take long for others to take notice of the great quality of fruit being produced by the one hungering and thirsting for righteousness.

For now, let it be sufficient to say that those of us who hunger and thirst for righteousness will truly be filled. We will begin to reap wondrous fruit and blessing in our lives as the prophet Hosea says, "Sow for yourselves in righteousness, reap the fruit of unfailing love, and break up your unplowed ground; for it is time to seek the LORD, until he comes and showers righteousness on you" (Hosea 10:12).

Insight #9: Righteousness and Faith

There we are, sitting in a café, drinking some coffee, and talking with a friend. Our conversation moves from talking about the weather, to our families, to remembering the old days. As we dwell upon the good times we had with one another, an old friend pops into both of our minds; one who was killed in a sudden car accident a few years ago. Our friend looks down at the table, slowly tapping his empty coffee cup against it, and then looks us in the eye saying, *"You know, it is kind of scary how quickly he was taken out of this world. If I die quickly like that, I sure hope my good deeds outweigh my bad deeds so I can get into Heaven."* How would we respond?

If it is by works we are saved none of us would be able to enter Heaven. Jesus says, "For I tell you that unless your righteousness surpasses that of the Pharisees and the teachers of the law, you will certainly not enter the kingdom of heaven" (Matthew 5:20). Jesus is not saying that a Pharisaical righteousness is going to save us, but rather that our righteousness has to be even greater than the Pharisees' to enter the Kingdom of Heaven. The Pharisees and teachers of the law appeared to do all the right things on the outside; they looked like good men; but still their righteousness was not good enough. The Lord says in Ezekiel, "The righteousness of the righteous man will not save him when he disobeys" (Ezekiel 33:12). With the exception of Jesus Christ, every single human being who has ever lived on the face of the earth has disobeyed God and given in to sin. Scripture is clear: "For all have sinned and fall short of the glory of God" (Romans 3:23).

No matter what we do or how hard we try, we cannot be good enough in and of ourselves to enter Heaven. Our righteousness is not righteous enough. Actually our righteousness, in God's eyes, is not even considered righteousness at all: "There is no one righteous, not even one" (Romans 3:10).

The apostle Paul understood that none of his own deeds would save him and that only one thing would grant him admission into Heaven—his faith in Christ. And Paul even recognized that his faith did not come from Himself but from God. He wrote in Philippians 3:9, ". . . not having a righteousness of my own that comes from the law, but that which is through faith in Christ—the righteousness that comes from God and is by faith." Paul also wrote, "For it is by grace you have been saved, through faith—and this not from yourselves, it is the gift of God—not by works, so that no one can boast" (Ephesians 2:8).

We are in such great need of the righteousness that comes from God, through Jesus Christ. Without the righteousness of Jesus Christ, we have nothing good in us. We can help as many people as we want, give all our money away, feed the hungry, care for the sick, go to church every single day of our lives and be on every church committee there is and still go to Hell for all of eternity if we are merely trusting in our own righteousness. Jesus' righteousness is true righteousness. When we believe in Jesus, He receives our sin and we receive His righteousness. Thanks be to God for the righteousness of Jesus Christ! Salvation does not come through anything we do. We do not have to become better people before we give our lives to Jesus. He wants us to come to Him as we are and receive His righteousness—become born again. Then, He will empower us to be the people He desires us to be, children in true obedience. The righteousness of God comes only through faith in Christ.

The righteousness of Jesus Christ is the only hope we have as believers. Scripture says, "But by faith we eagerly await through the Spirit the righteousness for which we hope" (Galatians 5:5). This verse is powerful when we allow the weight of it to penetrate our hearts. We as believers are placing all of our hope in the righteousness of Christ. His righteousness is the only thing we have to bank on. If the righteousness of Jesus Christ can't save us, there is no other hope anywhere; not in any other religion, not in the goodness of mankind, not in government, nor in the progress of modern technology. But the good news is that Jesus' righteousness can and will save us who believe. There truly is a heavenly kingdom awaiting us whose faith is in Christ. And, yes, we will be allowed to enter into this Kingdom because we have received the righteousness of Christ.

If we as believers still struggle over our own salvation, we need to honestly consider if we are placing our faith and hope in what we are doing or in the righteousness of Christ. Hungering and thirsting for righteousness has much to do with desiring a greater faith and hope in Christ's righteousness. Often, we are a people who like three step plans, something we can place our hands on, or something that we can see with our eyes. That is why, I believe, salvation is hard for so many of us. Too frequently Christians place the hope of their salvation in their walking down an isle at the end of a church service, or in their water baptism, or even in their repeating of a prayer at the end of a gospel tract. I have repeatedly talked to people who seem to show little evidence of being saved, yet when I share with them their need to surrender their all to Jesus, they reply, *"Oh, you don't need to worry about me. I got saved a long time ago. I made my peace with God. I'm good."* Salvation to them is something they have checked off their list of the many things they need to do in life. I can't help but wonder if they are truly placing their faith and hope in the righteousness of Christ or in some religious act they did for themselves a long time ago. Salvation comes through faith in Christ, and the evidence of our faith shows itself through the fruit of the rest of our lives.

I fully believe that if our one hope and faith is in the righteousness of Christ, we will hunger and thirst to understand His righteousness more and more. We will desire to explore the depths of Christ's righteousness and the greater truths of what His righteousness means for us now as believers. With that being the case, each of us as believers should seriously consider if we are placing too much emphasis in our own righteousness, treating our salvation as something we "already took care of" through the repeating of some words or through a religious ritual we did years ago. Let us strive, instead, to be someone who is constantly yearning for God to increase our faith and hope in Christ's righteousness, so much so, that we relentlessly go to God in prayer asking Him to reveal more and more of His truth to us through His word and asking for His Spirit to empower us to live in the fullness of Christ's righteousness in our daily lives.

Insight #10: Righteousness and Our Passion

So far, we have looked into nine insights regarding righteousness—believing God, justice, the Word of God, God's character, Jesus

Christ, believers, the Holy Spirit, fruit and faith. These concepts are what Jesus is referring to when He discusses hungering and thirsting for righteousness. With this in mind, we need to honestly evaluate whether we are ones who are hungering and thirsting for the things mentioned in the list above. Remember, as mentioned in chapter 2, that object which we hunger and thirst for is revealed to be our *passion*. So let us contemplate: Is believing God our passion? Is true godly justice our passion? Is the Word of God our passion? Is God's righteous character our passion? Are believers in Jesus Christ our passion? Is the fullness of the Holy Spirit our passion? Is the fruit of righteousness our passion? Is greater faith our passion?

To be passionate for these things is getting us closer to the meaning of hungering and thirsting for righteousness. And as these things begin to become our passion in increasing measure, we can be greatly encouraged by Jesus when He says, "Blessed are those who hunger and thirst for righteousness" (Matthew 5:6). Friends, our Lord and King says we are blessed when we are passionate for righteousness!

The Greek word for blessed (*makarios*) carries the idea of complete happiness in life, complete joy, contentedness and fullness of life.[20] Some of us may think we are blessed, content, joyful and happy in our current condition, but if we have never truly hungered and thirsted for righteousness we do not even comprehend what we are missing out on. If righteousness is not the one passion of our lives, then we have never actually understood or experienced true blessing, contentedness, joy and happiness. Once we experience and know the blessing that comes from our hungering and thirsting for righteousness, we will never desire to pursue or be distracted by anything else but righteousness. Therefore, it would be advantageous for each of us to reflect on whether or not we are a person who hungers and thirsts for righteousness in the sense described, and if we are truly experiencing God's pure gift of blessing, joy, contentment and happiness in our lives as He intends us to.

Once we have tasted the blessing of being passionate for righteousness, we will never try to satisfy our hunger and thirst anywhere else or in anything else. Let us allow the marvelous words of Psalm 34:8-10 soak into our hearts:

> Taste and see that the LORD is good; blessed is the man who takes refuge in him. Fear the LORD, you his saints, for those who fear him lack nothing. The lions may grow weak and hungry, but those who seek the LORD lack no good thing.

Jesus, understanding the goodness of God the Father and the Father's provision to give His children good things, urges anyone who will listen to Him, "seek first [God the Father's] kingdom and his righteousness" (Matthew 6:33). The righteousness of God is to be the passion of our hearts. And when we are passionate for the righteousness of God, we will be blessed.

The writer of Psalm 118 reveals his passion for God's righteousness, "Open for me the gates of righteousness; I will enter and give thanks to the LORD" (Psalm 118:19). How we need to have the same passion for righteousness as this psalmist! Let us be ones who cry out to God, *"Open for me the gates of righteousness and I will enter in. All thanks and glory be to You, Oh Lord!"* Our earnestness should be the same as the Lord God Almighty:

> You heavens above, rain down righteousness; let the clouds shower down. Let the earth open wide, let salvation spring up, let righteousness grow with it; I, the LORD, have created it (Isaiah 45:8).

If we become as passionate for righteousness as God is passionate for righteousness, we will see and experience the fullness of God in our lives in a way we have never known before. This does, however, raise a question. What does Jesus mean by saying that those who hunger and thirst for righteousness will be filled?

"O God, make us ones who throw up our hands to fully understand that we have nothing to offer You except Christ in us. Let us be ones who hunger and thirst to comprehend more of Christ's righteousness and what His righteousness means in our lives. Let us not be content to say, 'I'm saved' and then carry on with life as usual. You have given us the righteousness of Christ. What else do we have to place our faith in, or what other hope do we have? Thank You, thank You, thank You for the righteousness of Jesus Christ given to us! Now, let His righteousness be the one passion and pursuit of the rest of our lives. Amen."

6

You Will Be Filled

"The next best thing to living in the light of the Lord's love is to be unhappy till we have it, and to pant hourly after it—hourly, did I say? Thirst is a perpetual appetite, and not to be forgotten, and even thus continual is the heart's longing after God. When it is as natural for us to long for God as for an animal to thirst, it is well with our souls, however painful our feelings."[21]

- Charles H. Spurgeon

Sometimes we find ourselves at a loss for words. We try to describe something to someone, but just cannot find the right words to cause that person to fully grasp what we are saying. It is frustrating when other people do not understand us. Most of us have been to a breathtakingly, beautiful place, tried to capture the beauty of that place with a camera, but found as we showed the photos to our friends and family that the pictures were not nearly as captivating as the real thing. After our presentation we have to conclude by saying: *It is so amazing! You just have to go and experience it for yourself.* There are certain things that simply cannot be understood without first-hand experience.

I believe that Matthew 5:6 is one of these examples: "Blessed are those who hunger and thirst for righteousness, for they will be filled." For us to truly understand what Jesus means by saying "they will be filled," we just have to begin experiencing this for ourselves. We can read and study all we want about this subject, and we can talk to other believers day and night about it. But simply reading, studying and talking about this fullness Jesus speaks of in Matthew 5:6 cannot compare to actually receiving this fullness ourselves.

With that being said, it is still important to read, study and discuss what Jesus means to at least have some idea what it is He desires us to begin experiencing. I have heard it said, "*If we don't know where we are going, we will never know if we get there.*" We at least need some sort of idea in our minds and hearts what this *being filled* is all about so we can better comprehend the place to which Jesus is desiring to bring us as we begin to hunger and thirst for righteousness.

As we study and learn about this filling that Jesus mentions, let us not be satisfied with simply knowing about this subject. May we, instead, pray that God ignites, within our hearts, a desire to actually begin experiencing the full reality of what Jesus is teaching.

My wife and I were recently blessed to be able to take a trip to the land of Israel. To prepare our hearts and minds before we went, we looked at pictures, watched videos and talked with friends who had been to Israel. All of this made us more excited about going. However, even though these pictures, videos and discussions helped us understand more about Israel, these did not even compare to actually experiencing the land of Israel for ourselves. Similarly, as we continue in our discussion, may this be the spark we need to begin earnestly desiring this fullness Jesus speaks of to arise in our own lives. This discussion, of course, will pale in comparison to the fullness experienced once we begin hungering and thirsting for righteousness ourselves.

Never the Same

Certain events alter us for the rest of our lives. For my wife and me, the day our first child was born was one of those events. Suddenly our lives were completely different. Our family grew by a whole other person! No longer did we just have each other, but we also had a son as well. Our discussions changed; our thinking changed; our sleeping patterns changed; the way we spent our money changed; even our sympathy for other parents changed. Now, my wife and I have a total of three children, and neither one of us can really remember the quiet life when it was just the two of us. Our lives have changed dramatically.

This filling Jesus mentions in Matthew 5:6 is also life altering. The word which gets translated as *filled* in this verse comes from the Greek word "chortazō" which can mean to eat one's fill, be filled to satisfaction or be content.[22] The word used here is "a very strong and graphic word, originally applied to the feeding and fattening of animals in a stall. It is manifestly appropriate here as expressing the complete satisfaction of spiritual hunger and thirst."[23] Therefore, what Jesus is saying is that those who hunger and thirst for righteousness will be filled to complete satisfaction. Just as a domestic animal has all its food right there in front of him in the barn stall and can eat until he is completely satisfied, those who hunger and thirst for righteousness will have everything they need right in front of them and will be able to eat to their complete satisfaction.

The satisfaction Jesus mentions will bring dramatic change to every area of our lives. We will never be the same. Once we begin to experience this satisfaction, things will begin to happen. What do I mean by this? First, we need to realize that the only thing that can satisfy our hunger and thirst is to actually be filled with the thing for which we hunger and thirst. Therefore, if we hunger and thirst for righteousness, the only thing that will satisfy our hunger and thirst is to actually be filled with righteousness. As we know, our righteousness and our good works will not do; only the righteousness which comes from God will bring this satisfaction.

At the end of the day, people who try their hardest to be good and moral people through their own works and religion will still feel quite dissatisfied. Only those who are filled with the righteousness of God will be satisfied. Therefore, we must understand this satisfaction only begins as we recognize our desperate need for the righteousness of God. Our hunger and thirst for the righteousness of God will first be revealed through our crying out to Him in confession and repentance of our sins, asking His forgiveness and believing in our hearts Jesus Christ to be our Lord and Savior.

But what about the filling? With what exactly will those who hunger and thirst for the righteousness of God be filled or satisfied? According to God's word, when we repent of our sin and surrender our lives to Jesus, something greater takes place than just a mere decision to follow Jesus Christ. Jesus says, "I tell you the truth, no one can see the kingdom of God unless he is born again" (John 3:3). Jesus goes on to say, "I tell you the truth, no one can enter the kingdom of God unless he is born of water and the Spirit" (John 3:5). Becoming a believer is more than just taking on the title "Christian." Actually, to truly become a believer, we must be born again. The apostle Paul, in Romans 6, discusses how believers have died to sin and now are alive in Christ. Paul also explains in Galatians 6:15 how believers are actually a new creation. We are new creatures in Christ. The old is gone, the new has come. This newness comes not from ourselves, but from God as He places His Holy Spirit into us as believers. Anyone who is a believer, in the truest sense of the word, has the Holy Spirit of God living in them.[24] The filling has begun because the Holy Spirit now lives in us. We will never be the same.

Let the Filling Continue

Sadly, so many people stop at this point and think that since they have already confessed their sin, asked for forgiveness, and received Jesus as Lord and Savior that is the end of what God has for them. Now let me be extremely clear—I do not want to downplay our conversion by any means. Our becoming born again through Jesus Christ is the most important thing to ever happen to us. There is nothing else we need to do to be justified because Jesus has done everything for us. However, we as Christians must grow up in our salvation. Our becoming a Christian is not the end, but only the beginning. A baby does not stay a baby, but it grows and matures.

If we are in Christ, we have been born again. At the point of our conversion, we become a babe in Christ and the Holy Spirit comes into us. Maybe we can name the time and place this happened. Maybe we can describe some great feeling we had at the moment of our conversion. But what about now? Have we grown beyond the point where we started when we first believed?

When we became a new creature in Christ, our hunger and thirst for the righteousness of God may have been strong, and our passion for Jesus may have been great. Possibly, many years have passed since the time we gave our lives to Christ. How is our hunger and thirst now? Some of us might respond, *"I'm saved. It is all taken care of. What more is there?"* Well, God desires that we never stop hungering and thirsting for His righteousness. Even though we have already been forgiven of our sins and have already received the righteousness of Jesus, God has so much more in store for us. As great as is the grace and miracle of our salvation, God's plan is not just to get us into Heaven. He also calls us to live, right here, right now, in the righteousness of Jesus Christ which we received at our new birth.

Should we be satisfied with mediocrity? Shouldn't we want to know and experience more of God and His righteousness? Shouldn't we long to be satisfied by God, in a way greater than we've ever dreamed possible? Some of us might ask, *"Is it possible to become completely satisfied in this life?"* Honestly, I do not think so. I believe the more we hunger and thirst for the righteousness of God, the more we will see and experience this satisfaction going deeper and deeper and deeper still. But the choice is ours. Our satisfaction only goes as deep as our hunger and thirst for righteousness. May we never allow our hunger and thirst for righteousness to cease.

Filled in So Many Ways

The question still remains—what specifically does Jesus mean when He says, "they will be filled"? Once we become born again, God places His Holy Spirit into us. It is then up to us whether to live by the Spirit or by our sinful nature as the apostle Paul declares, "So I say, live by the Spirit, and you will not gratify the desires of the sinful nature" (Galatians 5:16).

The more we hunger and thirst for the righteousness of God, the more God will fill and satisfy us in increasing measure. Scripture says, "Now the Lord is the Spirit, and where the Spirit of the Lord is there is freedom. And we, who with unveiled faces all reflect the Lord's glory, are being transformed into his likeness with ever-increasing glory, which comes from the Lord, who is the Spirit" (2 Corinthians 3:17-18). How remarkable! We are being transformed into the likeness of our Lord Jesus Christ with ever-increasing glory.

The filling we receive as we hunger and thirst for righteousness has much to do with our becoming more like Jesus Christ. Becoming like the Righteous One in our thinking, our actions, our motives, our feelings, our outlook, our conversation, our trust, our everything. And as we become more like Jesus, those things which fill and satisfy Jesus will also begin to fill and satisfy us. Still though, we might wonder what it means to become more like Jesus and what those things are which fill and satisfy Him.

There are truths from Scripture about what begins to happen in the lives of the righteous. But before we explore those truths, I want to make myself clear. Even though we become righteous once we are born again, we must not think that this automatically means we suddenly begin living in the fullness of what God has for us. Being born again is just the beginning. From that point on, how much we experience the fullness and satisfaction God has for us is directly connected to our hunger and thirst for righteousness. The following will increase or decrease in our lives depending on our passion for the righteousness of God:

(1) *Filled with Light*
". . . let your light shine before men, that they may see your good deeds and praise your Father in heaven" (1 John 1:5-8).

Once we are born-again, we receive the light of Jesus Christ. However, simply because we have the light of Christ within us does not necessarily mean we are allowing this light to shine brightly. We must learn how to allow this light to shine brighter in our daily lives. The more we grow in our hunger and thirst for righteousness, the more our lives will overflow with the light of Jesus Christ, and the more we will be able to shine His light to the rest of the world.

This world is certainly full of people who are reflecting humanity's sinful nature. There are fewer and fewer people who are good examples for our children to imitate. We are in such great need of believers to overflow with the light of Jesus Christ in this broken and messed up world. What is the condition of our light? What would our family and friends say if they were asked how powerfully the light of Jesus is shining through us?

Righteousness and light go hand in hand. The book of Daniel says, "Those who are wise will shine like the brightness of the heavens, and those who lead many to righteousness, like the stars for ever and ever" (Daniel 12:3). To lead many people to righteousness, we must first greatly desire righteousness. If we are leading many to righteousness, it means we are shining the light of Christ immensely. It means we are filled with light overflowing and that others will sense Jesus Christ simply by our presence.

I pray that we so eagerly desire for our light to shine, we actually begin leading our families and friends to righteousness. But our hunger and thirst for righteousness needs to be great. May we as believers, be ones who overflow with the light already within us. This broken world has abundant need for each of us to shine.

(2) *Filled with the Holy Spirit*
"Then Peter, filled with the Holy Spirit, said to them . . ." (Acts 4:8).

"But Stephen, full of the Holy Spirit, looked up to heaven and saw the glory of God, and Jesus standing at the right hand of God" (Acts 7:55).

"[Barnabas] was a good man, full of the Holy Spirit and faith, and a great number of people were brought to the Lord" (Acts 11:24).

The question for us as believers is not do we have the Holy Spirit in us, but rather, are we living filled with the Holy Spirit? If we do not have the Holy Spirit in us, Scripture is clear—we are not born again. But even if we do have the Holy Spirit in us, this does not mean we are necessarily living in His fullness. Jesus' statement in Matthew 5:6 has much to do with living in the fullness of the Holy Spirit. As we have discovered, Galatians 5:16 urges us to "live by the Spirit, and we will not gratify the desires of the sinful nature." The choice is ours to live by the Spirit or to live according to our sinful nature. It is also written in Galatians, "Those who belong to Christ Jesus have crucified the sinful nature with its passions and desires. Since we live by the Spirit, let us keep in step with the Spirit" (Galatians 5:24-25). We as believers have crucified the sinful nature with its passions and desires, therefore, let us not go back. Those things are dead and there is no life in them at all. Yet there is life in the Spirit. We must keep in step with the Spirit by living in His fullness, which is, in many ways, connected to our hunger and thirst for righteousness.

If we are born again, we must know that we do in fact have the Holy Spirit in us. But we must also realize, just because we are born again does not necessarily mean we are living full of the Holy Spirit. Are we showing we want to experience the daily power of the Holy Spirit? Do our lives reveal that we want what Peter, Stephen and Barnabas had when Scripture says they were full of the Holy Spirit? If so, then we must be ones who hunger and thirst for righteousness. Only then does Jesus promise we will be filled.

The life of those who are full of the Holy Spirit will be characterized by the fruit of the Spirit: "love, joy, peace, patience, kindness, goodness, faithfulness, gentleness and self-control" (Galatians 5:22-23). What person does not long for these things to be manifested in their life? When men and women begin living in the fullness of the Holy Spirit, great and mighty things occur. The modern day church is in immense need of Christians to be in complete, total surrender to the Holy Spirit.

(3) *Filled with Holiness*

"I am the LORD your God; consecrate yourselves and be holy, because I am holy" (Leviticus 11:44).

"Therefore, O king, let my advice be acceptable to you; break off your sins by being righteous" (Daniel 4:27, New King James Version).

Perhaps there is sin in our lives of which we have difficulty letting go. God has called His people to holiness, to be holy as He is holy (Leviticus 11:44). The prophet Daniel gave king Nebuchadnezzar wise advice, "break off your sins by being righteous" (Daniel 4:27, NKJV). The sins we struggle with in this life begin breaking off as we begin living righteously. We cannot live righteously on our own. God must empower us to live righteously. All we can do is hunger and thirst for righteousness. And as we do, Jesus will empower us to break free from our sin. Jesus has come to set us free!

Our holiness is directly connected to our hunger and thirst for righteousness. Do we desire to be so completely free from that sin in our lives, with which we struggle so horribly, that we never give in to it again? Do we desire to be holy as God is holy and be filled with holiness? If so, then we must be passionate for righteousness and know that Jesus is saying to each of us personally, "Blessed are you who hunger and thirst for righteousness, for you will be filled" (Matthew 5:6). The more we hunger and thirst for righteousness, the more we will be filled with greater and greater holiness.

(4) *Filled with Fearlessness*

"In righteousness you will be established: Tyranny will be far from you; you will have nothing to fear. Terror will be far removed; it will not come near you" (Isaiah 54:14).

Those who are righteous have nothing to fear. Is a lion afraid of the dark? By no means! A lion walks confidently in the dark because he can see clearly. Similarly, we who are righteous have nothing to fear. Though the darkness may surround us, we must not fear, for we belong to the light. We have the righteousness of Jesus Christ within us; therefore, we have overcome the terrors of this world and, even more importantly, we no longer need to fear the wrath of God.

Jesus says, "Do not be afraid of those who kill the body but cannot kill the soul. Rather, be afraid of the One who can destroy both soul and body in hell" (Matthew 10:28). Once we have a proper fear of God, we will come to Him, recognizing that He is the only One we should fear because He holds all power and authority. As Proverbs 9:10 says: "The fear of the LORD is the beginning of wisdom." But once we have come to Jesus Christ, receiving His forgiveness and His righteousness, we must trust in God's grace. Those of us who belong to Jesus Christ will most assuredly enter into God's eternal Kingdom and do not need to fear eternal weeping and gnashing of teeth in Hell. We who are born again will never face God's wrath. We are secure because of the righteousness of Jesus Christ.

Scripture makes it clear that this world is not the home of the believer. We are not to get too comfortable here. We are to stand firm in our faith no matter what. We are to trust God and obey Him even if it costs us everything. Why? Because even if the worst troubles, persecutions and heartaches happen here in this life, these are nothing compared to the eternal blessings and glories of the Kingdom to come, the place where we will live for all eternity. Even if we lose everything in this life, we can rejoice in the reality that our reward will be great in Heaven. We have nothing to fear.

In reality, however, many Christians still live with some sense of fear. Many have a fear of the future, a fear of sickness, a fear of death, a fear for the safety of those they love or a fear of evil things happening. But why do so many of us fear the things of this world? Scripture says, "The LORD is with me; I will not be afraid. What can man do to me?" (Psalm 118:6). The Lord is with the righteous. The more we hunger and thirst for righteousness, the more we will grasp and understand the righteousness of Jesus Christ living in us and will be filled with greater and greater fearlessness. Nothing can come against us when we are in Christ, not even Satan himself. The righteous are secure. If we are driven by a sense of fear in our lives, then it is vital we grow in our hunger and thirst for righteousness, so that God may fill us with greater fearlessness.

(5) *Filled with Hope and Trust*
"But seek first his kingdom and his righteousness, and all these things will be given to you as well. Therefore do not worry about tomorrow, for tomorrow will worry about itself. Each day has enough trouble of its own" (Matthew 6:33).

Hope and trust go right along with fearlessness. If we hunger and thirst for righteousness, we have nothing to fear in this world, and we have everything to hope in. Jesus makes it clear that if our priorities are straight, meaning that God's Kingdom and God's righteousness are the first things we seek, we have absolutely nothing to worry about.

Sometimes we worry over matters we have no control over. Admittedly, I still do at times. But, as my passion for righteousness grows, God is constantly teaching me that He is in control of all things and I have no need to worry. God is a good God and a good Father. I am His child because I have been born again. The righteousness of Jesus Christ is within me. God takes care of His children. He will take care of my needs. What I think I need may not be what God knows I need. Therefore, I must trust that God knows what is best.

As we grow in our hunger and thirst for righteousness, our hope and trust in the goodness of God will grow as well. We will be filled with greater hope and trust in God until we come to the point where we will honestly be able to say with the apostle Paul, "And we know that in all things God works for the good of those who love him, who have been called according to his purpose" (Romans 8:28).

We, as God's people, should long to have a greater hope and trust in Him. Our passion for righteousness has much to do with the amount of hope and trust we have in God. May God increase our passion for His righteousness so that we cease worrying and begin to show greater hope and trust in Him in every situation.

(6) *Filled with Life*

"He who pursues righteousness and love finds life, prosperity and honor" (Proverbs 21:21).

"In the way of the righteous there is life; along that path is immortality" (Proverbs 12:28).

We have all heard someone say about another person, "*That person is full of life!*" What is often meant by that statement is the person is full of energy or making the most out of their life. Everyone has their opinion about what it means "to make the most out of life." But let us not trust our own opinion. Instead, let us go to the One who can be trusted, Jesus Christ Himself, as He says, "I have come that they may have life, and have it to the full" (John 10:10).

In Jesus there is life; not just more life or another version of life, but life in the truest and fullest sense. Jesus says, "I am the way, the truth and the life" (John 14:6). Jesus is not just the way and the truth, but He is also the life. When we come to Jesus Christ and become born again, we actually learn what it is to live for the first time.

Before we believe in Jesus, no matter what we may think, there is no life in us. We are dead in our sin. Unbelievers may think, *"I don't feel dead. Actually, I feel alive."* But how can someone who has always been dead know what it is to feel alive? Jesus has come to give us life and reveal to us what true life is all about. In Jesus there is *eternal* life. Eternal life does not simply mean we will go to Heaven when we die, but it means we begin living and experiencing this life right here and right now.

Some Christians seem to believe that when someone is born again they immediately begin experiencing the fullness of the life Jesus offers. But does a little baby experience the fullness of life the moment he is born? No. The baby grows and matures and learns more and more what life is all about. The same is true for the Christian. When we become born again, we come to life for the first time. But this does not necessarily mean we are yet living in the fullness of which Jesus is speaking.

Jesus has so much more life to reveal to us. The more we walk with Him and abide in Him, the greater we understand and experience this life Jesus speaks of in John 10:10, "I have come that they may have life, and have it to the full." Do we long to experience life in the deepest way Jesus offers? Let us not miss out on this full life Jesus has to offer and heed to the wisdom of the Proverbs, "In the way of the righteous there is life; along that path is immortality" (Proverbs 12:28).

Hungering and thirsting for the righteousness of God increases the fullness of our lives. It could honestly be said of those who are passionate for righteousness that they are ones who are full of life. Do we believe there to be more to *life in Christ* than what we are currently experiencing? Let us fall down on our knees and pray for God to increase our passion for His righteousness. If we do this, allowing this prayer to come from our hearts, then we will gradually begin to experience the fullness of life in a way grander than we ever before new existed. People all around us are in dire need for us to be filled with greater life.

(7) *Filled with Love*
"The LORD detests the way of the wicked but he loves those who pursue righteousness" (Proverbs 15:9).

Some of us have gone through times of questioning God's love. Sometimes we as believers have a hard time accepting God's personal love for us as individuals. We may think we have done too much wrong or feel we are too small and unimportant for God to really love us all that much. The truth is, however, God the Father loves us who believe—immeasurably. Scripture speaks to all believers, "How great is the love the Father has lavished on us, that we should be called children of God! And that is what we are!" (1 John 3:1).

Because of what Jesus Christ has done for us, when we are born again we are adopted into God's family. We who are now God's children have been forgiven of our sins and have received the righteousness of Jesus Christ. Since we are now in the family of God we need to understand that God is a good Father and He has a vast love for His children. God the Father loves His Son, Jesus; therefore, we who now have Jesus dwelling in us through the Holy Spirit can trust God's love for us as well. The apostle Paul writes of this great love God has for us who believe: "For I am convinced that neither death nor life, neither angels nor demons, neither the present nor the future, nor any powers, neither height nor depth, nor anything else in all creation, will be able to separate us from the love of God that is in Christ Jesus our Lord" (Romans 8:38–39).

Still, it is hard for many to accept God's infinite love for them. Could it be because so many of us are choosing to keep more in step with the ways of the world than with the Spirit of God? The book of Proverbs is clear, "The LORD detests the way of the wicked but he loves those who pursue righteousness" (Proverbs 15:9). Why do so many of us turn back to the way of the wicked and live in doubt, unbelief and weakness? Now that we have been made righteous, and we know God loves those who pursue righteousness, why would we want to go back and pursue the way of the wicked anymore? It makes no sense.

One looming reason so many of us question God's personal love for us is because our failure in the pursuit of righteousness causes our minds to be clouded to the truth. We must not pursue after the way of the wicked. We must pursue righteousness so that we know and understand God's great love for us.

God rejoices when we are passionate for righteousness and pursue righteousness with our whole being. The more passionate we are for righteousness, the more we will be filled with God's love, and the more we will have a greater understanding of His love. Only then will we begin to love the way God loves. Oh, that we would pursue righteousness and come to a greater understanding of God's love for us that we may in turn be filled more and more with the love of God! May we allow God to bring us to the place of loving what He loves and detesting what He detests.

(8) *Filled with Intimacy with God*
"You meet him who joyfully works righteousness, those who remember you in your ways." (Isaiah 64:5, English Standard Version).

There may be times when we go through seasons when we want to feel more of God's presence in our lives. We feel our relationship with God fading and wonder why it is so hard for us to hear God's voice. In these times, going through the motions of our religious traditions or trying to earn God's favor by our performance is not what we want. Nor do we want to simply read *about* God. Instead, we want God's real presence in our lives. We yearn for a deeper relationship with God. Intimate relationship with God is what Christianity is all about.

When it comes down to it, probably every Christian has some desire to have a stronger relationship with God than they currently have. Some have a stronger desire than others, but I believe most Christians would admit their relationship with God needs to be stronger. Many of us, however, do not quite understand how to obtain a stronger relationship with God.

The prophet Isaiah writes, "You meet with him who joyfully works righteousness, those who remember you in your ways" (Isaiah 64:5, ESV). Living righteously and intimacy with God go hand in hand. No, we do not work our way to God. However, God does desire us to seek that for which we are looking for. He will not force us to come to Him, but He does urge us to draw near to Him. If we do, He will in turn draw near to us. The book of James shares how our drawing near to God and our living righteous and pure lives are inseparable:

> Submit yourselves, then, to God. Resist the devil, and he will flee from you. Come near to God and he will come near to you. Wash your hands, you sinners, and purify your hearts, you double-minded. Grieve, mourn and wail. Change your laughter to mourning and your joy to gloom. Humble yourselves before the Lord, and he will lift you up (James 4:7-8).

As we hunger and thirst for righteousness, we will be filled with greater intimacy with God. The more we are passionate for righteousness the more God will meet with us, speak with us, share His heart with us, and let us feel as He feels and see as He sees. As Isaiah 64:5 says, God meets with the one who joyfully works righteousness, which means someone who actually loves and enjoys righteousness. This paints a picture in my mind of someone who just can't seem to get enough, in other words, one who hungers and thirsts for righteousness.

God desires to meet with us in deep intimacy. But He will only meet with us if we desire to *meet* with Him. God greatly desires to share His heart and His deepest thoughts with us. Maybe we think we already know God's heart and His thoughts because we know the Bible so well. If that is the case, we must know that although it is extremely important to know and understand the teachings of Scripture, the intimacy God desires us to have with Him goes beyond mere knowledge. He desires us to actually begin feeling and even sharing the intensity of His heart.

When we begin sharing in the intensity of God's heart, we begin to weep for those things that break God's heart. We begin to shout for joy over the things that make God joyful. We begin hating with a holy hatred those things God hates. We begin to feel the deep and passionate love God feels for people. We begin doing those things He desires us to do instead of just doing whatever we think best. We begin to better understand what Jesus meant when He said, "I tell you the truth, the Son can do nothing by himself; he can do only what he sees his Father doing, because whatever the Father does the Son also does." The greater our intimacy with God, the greater our inability to live in disobedience will be.

Do we want to be filled with greater intimacy with God? Our passion for righteousness has much to do with the depth of our intimacy with God. Let us be challenged to cry out to God, day after day, for Him to increase our passion for righteousness. As we do, He will answer our prayer. We will then begin to experience an intimacy with God deeper than we ever knew was possible.

(9) *Filled with a Longing for Heaven*

"Now there is in store for me the crown of righteousness, which the Lord, the righteous Judge, will award me on that day—and not only to me, but also to all who have longed for his appearing" (2 Timothy 4:8).

The apostle Paul had an intense longing for Heaven, which is revealed in his writing to the Philippian church, "I desire to depart and be with Christ, which is better by far; but it is more necessary for you that I remain in the body" (Philippians 1:23-24). The more we hunger and thirst for righteousness, the more we will long for the coming of God's Kingdom. This world is fading and is full of sin, corruption, decay, and evil. There is a spiritual battle warring around us all the time. We, as God's people, are to always be armed and ready in the midst of this warfare.[25] This battle can be exhausting at times, and we need to be armed and ready to fight on a daily basis; every second of every day. It is even waged within our own hearts and minds. How wonderful it will be when the war is over.

As we hunger and thirst for righteousness, we ourselves begin seeing and understanding the complete beauty and goodness of righteousness. We will then greatly desire for all things to be made new; to be made righteous. We will be fervent for the day when all sin and all evil are done away with once and for all, and live in persistent eagerness of receiving the fullness of our righteousness in Jesus Christ. The apostle Paul understood to the anticipation of Heaven,

> Now there is in store for me the crown of righteousness, which the Lord, the righteous Judge, will award me on that day—and not only to me, but also to all who have longed for his appearing (2 Timothy 4:8).

How much do we long for Heaven? Our passion for righteousness impacts how much we desire Heaven. The stronger our desire for Heaven, the stronger our desire to live righteously becomes. Randy Alcorn, in his book *HEAVEN* speaks of this truth:

> Christ-centered righteous living today is directly affected by knowing where we're going and what rewards we'll receive there for serving Christ. After all, if we really believe we're going to live forever in a realm where Christ is the center who brings joy, and that righteous living will mean happiness for all, why wouldn't we choose to get a head start on Heaven through Christ-centered righteous living now?[26]

As we begin to hunger and thirst for righteousness, we will be filled with a longing for Heaven that can only be compared to homesickness. Our desire to receive the crown of righteousness will grow more and more intense. Our yearning to be with our Lord Jesus Christ will increase. Our lives, in the here and now, will begin to reflect the righteous lives we will live one day in Heaven. Do we long for Heaven as we should?

(10) *Filled with Persecution*
"Blessed are those who are persecuted for the sake of righteousness, for theirs is the kingdom of heaven" (Matthew 5:10).

"In fact, everyone who wants to live a godly life in Christ Jesus will be persecuted" (2 Timothy 3:12).

"Remember the words I spoke to you: 'No servant is greater than his master.' If they persecuted me, they will persecute you also" (John 15:20).

Okay, some people might think, "*I don't really want my life to be filled with persecution.*" But still, we must look at all the Bible says; not just the parts that make us comfortable. Jesus is very clear, "If they persecuted me, they will persecute you also" (John 15:20). The more we hunger and thirst for righteousness, the more we become like Jesus, and therefore, the more we will face persecution as He did.

Jesus says, "Everyone who does evil hates the light, and will not come into the light for fear that his deeds will be exposed" (John 3:20). The darkness detests the light. Those who belong to this sinful world hate the light that the righteous shine. The righteous will face persecution in all forms in this world—they may be mocked, laughed at, ridiculed, thought of as silly, gossiped about, falsely accused, treated unfairly, tested, threatened, beaten, tortured or even killed. The more we hunger and thirst for righteousness, the more we will be faced with persecution from the world.

But there is good news. This persecution will actually be to our joy. This sounds crazy, but look at what Jesus says in Matthew 5:10-12:

> Blessed are those who are persecuted because of righteousness, for theirs is the kingdom of heaven. Blessed are you when people insult you, persecute you and falsely say all kinds of evil against you because of me. Rejoice and be glad, because great is your reward in heaven, for in the same way they persecuted the prophets who were before you.

When we are persecuted for the sake of righteousness, we can rejoice and be glad because our reward will be great in Heaven. The book of 1 Peter also urges us to rejoice when we are persecuted, "But rejoice that you participate in the sufferings of Christ, so that you may be overjoyed when his glory is revealed" (1 Peter 4:13).

The greater our passion for righteousness, the greater our persecution in this world will be. However, as we become more and more like Jesus through His righteousness, we will at the same time experience an increased joy in the midst of this persecution as we realize this world is not our home. Our home, as believers, is in Heaven. How great our reward will be in our eternal home when we are persecuted. Persecution and trouble in this life actually loosens our grip on this world and increases our desire for the world to come.

Suffering for the sake of Christ also means we will experience, in a greater way, the power of God; the kind that the apostle Paul speaks of, "I want to know Christ and the power of his resurrection and the fellowship of sharing in his sufferings" (Philippians 3:10). Paul wanted to know and experience Jesus Christ and His power in a way that few have, even though it meant he would have to suffer. Do we desire to be worthy enough to share in the fellowship of Jesus' sufferings? As we grow in our hunger and thirst for righteousness, we will begin to be filled, in increasing measure, with the great honor of suffering with Jesus in His persecution.

Genuine Peace and Rest

In Chapter 5, we looked at ten different insights into what righteousness is all about. One of those insights discussed righteousness and fruit. Isaiah 32:17 says, "The fruit of righteousness will be peace;

the effect of righteousness will be quietness and confidence forever." Let us remember, hungering and thirsting for righteousness means that we greatly desire to bear the fruit of righteousness in our lives— the complete "peace of God, which transcends all understanding" (Philippians 4:7). The filling which Jesus mentions in Matthew 5:6, and all that is present in Chapter 6, can be summed up in one word—PEACE.

When we begin hungering and thirsting for righteousness, the peace of God, which transcends all understanding will indeed begin to fill our lives. Yes, we will begin to be filled in the many different ways already discussed, but as we are increasingly filled as we continue living more and more righteously, the peace of God will slowly but surely come upon us in a powerful and mighty way, causing in us the quietness and confidence that Isaiah 32:17 points out.

Isaiah 32:17 first tells us that the fruit of righteousness is peace. This means that as those who hunger and thirst for righteousness actually begin living more righteously, they will in turn be filled with a peace coming from God. Righteous living results in the fruit of peace. This is the overarching point Jesus is making when He says, "for they will be filled" in Matthew 5:6.

The term that Isaiah 32:17 uses for peace carries many different meanings such as prosperity, completeness, safeness, health and well-being, satisfaction and contentment.[27] In other words, those who hunger and thirst for righteousness will truly begin to be filled with eternal prosperity, a completeness, a real security, a true well-being, a whole satisfaction and a contentment nothing in this world can compare to. This is the peace that Jesus promises for those who hunger and thirst for righteousness. No wonder He calls them blessed! They are blessed indeed with a peace which is out of this world—a Heavenly and God-given peace.

Isaiah 32:17 goes on to tell us the effect of righteousness is quietness and confidence. The Hebrew word translated as quietness can also mean to be at rest or to be calm.[28] The Hebrew word translated as confidence carries the idea of feeling safe and secure or walking in safety.[29] Therefore, the one who hungers and thirsts for righteousness will be filled with the peace of God and that peace will actually bring them to the point of experiencing real rest, calmness, safety and confidence.

Some of us are tired and feel like we are becoming extremely worn out. There may be times in our lives when we question if real peace, rest and security exist. But let us not think that we cannot personally experience those things in our present circumstances. Jesus says we can. He says, "Blessed are those who hunger and thirst for righteousness, for they will be filled" (Matthew 5:6). As we become passionate for righteousness, God will fill us in so many ways. He will make us more and more like Jesus Himself and ultimately this will lead to the everlasting peace of God resulting in REAL quietness, rest, safety and confidence in our lives.

Precious Rest

In the Old Testament we can read about the Sabbath Rest and God's continual emphasis in honoring the Sabbath Rest. For the purposes of this book, there is no time to go into detail about this topic. However, the Sabbath Rest is ultimately fulfilled in and through Jesus Christ. This is why Jesus says,

> Come to me, all you who are weary and burdened, and I
> will give you rest. Take my yoke upon you and learn from
> me, for I am gentle and humble in heart, and you will find

rest for your souls. For my yoke is easy and my burden is light (Matthew 11:28-30).

God desires His people to find true peace and rest. This peace and rest begins to fill our lives as we begin hungering and thirsting for righteousness. As our passion for righteousness increases, our realization of our desperate need for Jesus, the Righteous One, increases. We are hopelessly weary and powerless without Jesus. Jesus is our everything. Jesus is our very life source. Jesus gives us real peace, rest and satisfaction.

Who of us does not long for peace and rest? Yet, we may still be busying ourselves with going through the motions of life, church, religion, work and taking care of our daily affairs. If we are feeling exhausted and overwhelmed, Jesus is saying to us, *"Come to me. I will give you rest."* In the next chapter, let us continue this conversation about the satisfying peace and rest Jesus offers.

7

Eternally Satisfied

"Go on, in a full pursuit of all the mind that was in Christ, of inward and then outward holiness; so shall you be not almost but altogether, a Christian; so shall you finish your course with joy: You shall awake up after his likeness, and be satisfied."[30]

- John Wesley

Being a pastor gives me the blessed opportunity to minister to and counsel all sorts of different people. Though I have only been a pastor for a few years, I have already come to the conclusion that a large percentage of people feel as if there must be more to life than what they are currently experiencing. Many, battling this longing for something more, grow depressed as they concede in their own minds that this longing is simply a fanciful dream never to be fulfilled. There are so many people who feel like giving up, throwing in the towel and ending the mundane drudgery of their lives.

At one time, I counseled with a woman who was suffering from severe depression. She did not have a horrible life by any means, maybe not as good as some, but still better than many. She had a husband who was concerned about her. She had friends she could go to for help. She had people who reached out to her trying to show her love. But this woman, caught in her depression, was like a wave in the ocean being tossed about. Some days she would be happy. Other times she would be suicidal. I prayed with her, rebuked the enemy's work in her life and urged her to surrender her entire life to Jesus Christ. She confessed that she did pray a few times to God, and it just didn't seem to work. She still felt depressed. She wanted a quick fix. She tried all sorts of different things to help. Yet, she claimed that nothing she tried relieved her depression. She even claimed she tried God and He didn't work, but honestly I question whether she ever gave God a chance. I also question whether she truly hungered and thirsted for God. It seems she was going to God hoping to get a quick fix, but since she felt she did not immediately receive that from Him, she simply moved on and tried to quiet her dissatisfaction elsewhere.

Why are there more and more people growing depressed and dissatisfied in our day? So many people feel a void in their lives, minds and hearts. There are so many whose lives are characterized not by peace and rest but rather by extreme weariness and burden. And many who struggle with discontentment do not even know why they feel this way. They just know that they want this awful feeling gone. Unfortunately, our culture feeds off this dissatisfaction and has devised its own temporary cures for this emptiness.

We too often and too quickly seek after these worldly remedies as a temporary antidote for our dissatisfaction instead of coming to the One who promises to give us complete and eternal satisfaction. Some have said, *"Yeah, I tried God. He didn't work."* But I wonder how many people have actually come to God, sat at His feet and pleaded with Him to fill their lives with His peace and rest. How many of the people who have said, "*I tried God*" have ever honestly hungered and thirsted for His righteousness?

The problem does not lie with God, but in our desire. Is our desire to have a quick and easy fix to our problem so we can continue in our lives as usual, or do we desire to have our feeling of dissatisfaction and depression gone—once and for all—never to return again? If we want the latter of the two, are we willing to take the arduous and costly journey to everlasting satisfaction and peace? Jesus says, "Blessed are those who hunger and thirst for righteousness, for they will be filled" (Matthew 5:6). Hungering and thirsting for righteousness is not necessarily the "easy road" in this life, but it is the road which leads to everlasting satisfaction and peace. And as mentioned in the previous chapter, this hungering and thirsting for righteousness ultimately means desperately desiring Jesus Christ, the Righteous One, above anything and everything else this world has to offer.

Come to Jesus and Be Satisfied

The Gospel of John is one of my favorite books in the Bible. I love the accounts of Jesus which John chose to include in this book. One of these accounts, in John chapter 6, is extremely valuable in our quest to comprehend where genuine satisfaction is found.

Jesus Fills a Need
John 6:1–15

Take a moment and read John 6:1–15. In this text, Jesus is becoming more and more popular in His ministry. People are coming out of the woodwork to listen to Him and see what He will do next. John 6:2 states that, "a great crowd of people followed [Jesus] because they saw the miraculous signs he performed on the sick." Notice the reason why this crowd is following Jesus. They are following Him because of the miraculous signs He has performed.

Jesus obviously knows why this crowd is following Him, but still He is moved by the people's hunger. In fact, He is so moved that He actually performs another miracle by turning five small loaves of bread and two fish into a feast large enough to feed over five thousand people! Could you imagine being there and witnessing this first hand? This man does not just offer some good advice, but He actually physically and miraculously provides food as well.

The crowd is so enthralled by this wonder that they say, "Surely this is the Prophet who is to come into the world" (John 6:14). They had been hungry, and Jesus physically filled their bellies with food; and now, they do not want Him to leave. They are convinced Jesus is the Prophet prophesied to come, and they begin to think they need to take matters into their own hands. They want to make certain Jesus becomes their king, even if they have to force Him to take this position. And Jesus, knowing their intentions, withdraws to a mountain by himself (John 6:15).

This crowd is fixed upon the physical miracle of food provided for them. They start to believe that Jesus is in fact the One who can meet all of their needs; and they want Jesus to do it in their way and in their timing. If He does not agree to be their king, they will make Him do it. Not because they love Him, but because He meets their physical needs. But Jesus withdraws from them because what they want is so much less than what they ultimately need. Their way is not God's way.

We need to be extremely careful not to behave like this crowd. Let us not attempt to *force* Jesus to do something that He Himself does not have in mind. We won't be able to anyways. There may be times when we get aggravated at Jesus for not operating the way we think best or for not giving us what we think He should. But instead of getting distressed, we must trust that His way is considerably greater than our own ideas of what we think is best. Our attention must be fixed upon Jesus, the Miracle Maker, more than upon what we want Him to do for us. It is not the temporary miracles we should desire or focus upon—but it is Jesus.

"Jesus, Please Do This For Me!"
John 6:16-24

Reflect upon the words of John 6:16-24 for a moment. The multitude of people attempt to make Jesus king by force, so Jesus goes off to be by Himself. Jesus probably already told His disciples to go to Capernaum and that He would meet them there later. So after Jesus withdraws, the disciples get into a boat and set off for Capernaum. While they are sailing, Jesus actually walks on the water to the disciples (which would be an amazingly strange thing to see in and of itself), gets into the boat with them, and then immediately they arrive in Capernaum. Meanwhile, the crowd is left on the other side of the shore where Jesus had previously miraculously fed them. They are wondering where Jesus has gone off to, so they get into some boats and set sail for Capernaum in search of Him (John 6:24).

Some of us, as parents, have tried to "hide" from our children before. There we are, trying to have some time all alone where we can think, pray or just relax. Out of nowhere, a child comes running into the room bombarding us with a bunch of "why" questions or whining about wanting a snack or screaming that their brother or sister hit them. We try to be patient as we tell them to go play in another room. After a bit of arguing, they eventually give in and go play in their room. We then think to ourselves, *"Ah, quietness, very nice."* That is, until about ten seconds later when another child comes running in again asking us something else. In these moments we seriously contemplate—*"Can I just have a few seconds alone?"*

Quite possibly, in John 6, Jesus is wondering a similar thing. Jesus goes all the way to Capernaum, away from the crowd but they will not leave Him alone. They keep following Him; even getting into boats to go look for Him. They are like lost sheep. I am sure they are thinking something like, *"We were sick and Jesus healed us. We were hungry and Jesus fed us. We can't let Him get away! We have to take matters into our own hands. Surely this man is the Prophet prophesied to come; therefore we have to make Him our king! That is our desire . . . and we want our desire filled—right now."*

These people think they know what is most important. They think the best thing to happen at that moment is to make Jesus an actual, physical king in *their* kingdom. They do not have a clue what they are doing. They are not thinking with clear minds.

This makes me think about a certain occasion between Peter and Jesus. In Matthew 16:21, Jesus explained to His disciples how He was going to be killed and then raised to life on the third day. After Jesus revealed this, Peter took Jesus aside and rebuked Him saying, "Never, Lord! This shall never happen to you!" (Matthew 16:22). What Jesus said next, I'm sure, made Peter tremble. Jesus turned to Peter, probably looked him straight in the eye, and made a bold and firm statement, "Get behind me, Satan! You are a stumbling block to me; you do not have in mind the things of God, but the things of men" (Matthew 16:23).

What Peter did is similar to what the crowd is doing in John 6. They want an earthly king. They think they know what is best, just as Peter thought he knew what was best. Peter thought from the perspective of his momentary desire. The crowd of people in John 6 is also thinking from the perspective of their momentary desire.

Satan himself, at Jesus' temptation, showed Jesus all the kingdoms of the world and their splendor and told Jesus, "All this I will give you, if you will bow down and worship me" (Matthew 4:9). Jesus then immediately commanded Satan to leave Him alone (Matthew 4:10a). Is not this great crowd of people, in John 6, trying to get Jesus to do exactly what Satan wanted Him to do; to begin ruling as king right there and then? They are attempting to fulfill the Scriptures by making Jesus their king, but they actually have in mind the things of Satan, not God.

You and I have so much to learn from this crowd of people. How many times do we do things as individuals and as churches without really taking the time to pray and consider what God wants us to do? Often we assume we already know what God wants us to do and so we make our plans, ask God to bless them, and then move ahead with our own agendas. What if God Himself revealed that many of our plans were not actually what He wanted us to be doing in the first place or that they were not being done in the manner He wanted? How horrible and humbling that would be. We so often want Jesus to bless our great church programs; want to attract the crowds; want to see great miracles, signs, wonders and healings performed right here and now; want to see big and glorious things happen for our community. We are often quick to figure out what we want to see happen, and then we strive so hard to fulfill this in the way we think is best.

Now I am not trying to say that God has called us to sit back and do nothing. However, I am saying we must not assume that every apparent good deed we do as believers or as a church is necessarily what God desires of us at that moment. We so often see a need, jump up and go try to meet that need in our own power before we seek the Lord in intense prayer. Sure, all of us as Christians will admit God's people need to pray, but too many of us find it extremely hard to actually sit still and pray. We must not assume we already know what we need to do *until* we ask God what it is He wants us to do.

This is what the crowd does in John 6. They think they know what needs to be done when all the while Jesus has something greater in store that they do not even comprehend. They actually, unknowingly, are going against God's plans.

How many confessing Christians and how many churches in the United States are actually doing what God desires them to be doing? How many people are unknowingly going against God's plans, assuming they already know what God wants them to be doing?

If we are having trouble sitting still in earnest prayer before doing something, we may very well act in a way that goes against God's desires. The great crowd, in John 6, wants to act quickly to what they think is best. They want a desire fulfilled that they believe will bring the greatest satisfaction and fulfillment. What they do not understand is that Jesus has something greater in mind. Let us, in our day and time, be careful not to make the same mistake.

Food That Spoils
John 6:25-27

Now take a look at John 6:25-27. Once the crowd finds Jesus on the other side of the lake, they ask Him, "Rabbi, when did you get here?" (Matthew 6:25). Instead of answering their question, Jesus responds by saying, "I tell you the truth, you are looking for me, not because you saw miraculous signs but because you ate the loaves and had your fill" (Matthew 6:26). These people are no longer following Jesus because they see the miraculous signs He has performed on the sick (Matthew

6:2), instead they are now following Jesus because He actually has filled a real desire within their own personal lives. They were hungry, and Jesus provided food for them. But Jesus strongly urges them, "Do not work for food that spoils, but for food that endures to eternal life, which the Son of Man will give you" (Matthew 6:27).

I have witnessed time and time again a similar cycle in the lives of a great number of people. The cycle begins with a particular individual (*let's call this individual Sarah*) going through a difficult period in her life. It could be depression, a financial problem, a sickness, a dying loved one, or some other sort of difficulty. In Sarah's grief, she begins meeting frequently with a minister and other Christians to pour out her problems. She takes their advice and prays often to Jesus about her situation. She also starts gathering with the church on a more regular basis while she is in this crisis in her life. Then, what seems to be out of nowhere, something spectacular happens in Sarah's life. She experiences an answer to her prayers and begins to be more joyful. In her excitement, she praises God and testifies to others how she is growing stronger in the Lord. But soon afterwards, Sarah's desire to grow in the Lord begins to fade. She isn't nearly as excited about Jesus as she used to be. She stops going to church, stops reading the Bible and does not pray as much as she used to. Her life is once again going seemingly smooth.

Sarah seemed to desire Jesus during her trial. But once Jesus met her need, she became temporarily satisfied. She eventually went back to where she began, allowing the busyness of her life to distract her from what was most important. Sarah never really desired Jesus, rather she wanted Jesus to meet a temporary necessity she had. Once Jesus did that, she really didn't feel a need for Him anymore.

Sound familiar? Of course it does! It happens all of the time. I believe the problem lies in the fact that so many people have a greater desire for the temporary blessings in their life than they do for Jesus Himself. Too often people want an immediate physical or emotional desire to be filled, Jesus actually fills that desire when they need Him to, and then they feel satisfied. He has come to them in their time of crisis. They are temporarily satisfied, and this causes them to begin pushing Jesus aside. They feel they have received everything they wanted for the time being. And they will not truly turn to Jesus again until they feel they *need* Him to help them through another crisis.

If we are ones simply following Jesus because we desire for our lives to be comfortable; or because we want some immediate physical and emotional appetite to be filled; or because we want some temporary blessing right now in our lives—then we are acting just like the crowd in John 6. We are following Jesus for the simple reason that through Him we want our fill. We don't really desire Jesus or the things that Jesus desires for us, but rather we just want an instant satisfaction. We want to see Jesus do something; to meet our need right here, right now.

We must move beyond this cycle of simply wanting Jesus to meet our every small desire and then when our desire is met just throwing Jesus aside until we need Him again. We must understand if we would only stay near to Jesus, He would satisfy us in a greater way than we ever imagined possible. All those small desires we once had would seem so insignificant in light of what Jesus really has in store for us. Why would we be satisfied with anything less?

My wife once shared with me a story she heard from a particular pastor. He told how he was going to surprise his children by taking them to a restaurant filled with pizza, entertainment, games and prizes—a kid's paradise. However, he did not tell his children where he was taking them. He just told them to get into the car because he had a surprise for them. As they were making their way to their surprise, they passed a fast food joint with one of those playgrounds attached to the side of it. The children saw the little playground and cried out, *"We want to go play at the playground at that food place."* He then said to his children, *"The place I am going to take you is WAY better than that little playground."* But the children insisted, *"No! We want to go to the playground!"* As the children continued to whine, he gave in to his children's desire. They wanted the little playground at the fast food joint, and that is exactly what they got. He decided not to take his children to the kid's paradise. After they ate at the fast food joint, they went home. His children never knew the immense fun and joy they missed out on. They were unwilling to trust that their dad had something greater in store for them. They were not patient and enduring in their wait, but rather they were content settling for their small desire to be filled. If only they would have waited and stayed the course, they would have experienced something so much better.

Do we not sometimes do a similar thing with God? Why do we as Christians settle for temporary satisfactions which fade and spoil rather than the increasing satisfaction enduring to eternal life? God has greater things in store for us that we do not yet comprehend.

Lasting Satisfaction
John 6:28-59

Look at John 6:28-59 and meditate upon the precious words of Jesus. In John 6:27, Jesus tells the crowd, "Do not work for food that spoils, but rather for food that endures to eternal life, which the Son of Man will give you." If we were there with this crowd in John 6, we would probably be wondering the same thing, "What must we do to do the works God requires?" (John 6:28). Jesus informs them the only work they need to do is to believe in the One that God has sent (John 6:29). The crowd, most likely understanding that Jesus is referring to Himself, wants a sign showing He is speaking the truth. What this crowd wants is something like the manna the Israelites received as they wandered in the wilderness (see Exodus 16:4). They want something physical they can see for themselves. Jesus tells them that His Father in Heaven has something greater than manna. The Heavenly Father has bread which comes down from Heaven and gives life to the world (John 6:33). If Jesus did not have the crowd's attention before, He has their attention now. They desperately want this bread Jesus is talking about. But here is where it gets interesting. Jesus blows them all away by making this statement, "I am the bread of life. He who comes to me will never go hungry, and he who believes in me will never be thirsty" (John 6:35).

I am sure some of the people in the crowd are probably thinking, "*Uh . . . what did Jesus just say? I think Jesus has flipped his lid.*" In John 6:41 some of the Jews are arguing and grumbling over Jesus' bold statement. Some of the Jews are even asking each other, "Is this not Jesus, the son of Joseph, whose father and mother we know? How can he now say, 'I came down from heaven'? (John 6:42)" But Jesus never backs down. Listen to what Jesus says in John 6:44-51,

> No one can come to me unless the Father who sent me draws him, and I will raise him up at the last day. It is written in the Prophets: "They will all be taught by God." Everyone who listens to the Father and learns from him comes to me. No one has seen the Father except the one who is from God; only he has seen the Father. I tell you the truth, he who believes has everlasting life. I am the bread of life. Your forefathers ate the manna in the desert, yet they died. But here is the bread that comes down from

heaven, which a man may eat and not die. I am the living bread that came down from heaven. If anyone eats this bread, he will live forever. This bread is my flesh, which I will give for the life of the world.

Jesus goes on to say in John 6:53–58,

I tell you the truth, unless you eat the flesh of the Son of Man and drink His blood, you have no life in you. Whoever eats my flesh and drinks my blood has eternal life, and I will raise him up at the last day. For my flesh is real food and my blood is real drink. Whoever eats my flesh and drinks my blood remains in me, and I in him. Just as the living Father sent me and I live because of the Father, so the one who feeds on me will live because of me. This is the bread that came down from heaven. Your forefathers ate manna and died, but he who feeds on this bread will live forever.

We have two options to consider here. Either Jesus has lost His mind, or He is revealing one of the most precious truths ever known to mankind. Many of the Jews who hear Jesus speak this no doubt think He is crazy. However, Jesus is not crazy, but rather He is speaking the truth of God. In Jesus is something exceptionally greater than a mere immediate, passing and temporary satisfaction. In Jesus is a satisfaction so great that we will never hunger or thirst for anything ever again. That, my friends, is a satisfaction we should want dearly.

Think about this: When we are physically hungry, we go and get something to eat, and we are immediately satisfied. When we are physically thirsty, we go and get something to drink and, again, we are immediately satisfied. But we will get hungry again, and we will get thirsty again. Jesus, on the other hand, offers us something which will cause us to never hunger or thirst again.

As people, we try to find satisfaction in so many different things. Often this quest occurs in a familiar type of cycle. Consider this:

> When we are in high school, we can't wait to graduate. Our great desire is to just get done with school. But after we graduate, we don't really feel completely satisfied. Then we think, *"Well, if I can just get a job, maybe then I'll be happy."* So we pray for God to get us a job. Our prayers are eventually answered as a job opens for us. Things go good for a little while, but it is not too long before we begin to think, *"I'm bored. At least this job pays the bills, but it really isn't as great as I thought it would be."* So we start looking for something else to satisfy us. Then, we think, *"Maybe if I was in a relationship with someone and got married, then I'd be satisfied."* So we pray for God to send us that special someone. Eventually, that prayer is answered and we get married. We are happy for awhile. But still, after a few years we continue to feel a sense of longing in our hearts. Then, we begin to think, *"Maybe we should have kids."* So, we have kids, and we are once again happy for the moment. But as years pass, our kids start growing up, and we feel we need something else to satisfy us. During this time we do upgrades to our houses, we buy new cars, we get more money, and we put money away in our retirement. We know we need to lift these things up in prayer to God and so we pray for Him to help with our job, our marriage, our kids, our houses, our finances, our decisions. And the cycle continues.

Don't misunderstand; it is vital that we lift each of these things up to the Lord in prayer. We must lift everything up to God in prayer.

But here is my point: While all of these things can be good desires, could it be that there is more to life than constantly wanting God to fulfill these kinds of immediate desires over and over again in our lives? Is there more to life than just getting a momentary answer to these desires, and then simply moving on, hoping to have another desire be temporarily satisfied? Are we just reacting to what we think we need, begging God over and over again to fill us in these ways as we allow these immediate desires we have to consume the majority of our prayer lives? None of those aforementioned things are necessarily bad, but could it be that God has more for us as believers than just repeating this cycle, over and over again?

Just as Jesus told the crowd, they were looking for Him because they had their fill (John 6:26), do we not sometimes follow Jesus simply to have our fill? Are we following Jesus because we know He can help us out with all of the instantaneous desires we have in this life? We often run to and fro from this small want to that small want, ask God to bless us with these things, but when He does, we never really seem completely satisfied. We often say we are glad and joyful about how much God has blessed us, and we give thanks to Him, but we would have to admit we still don't feel wholly content. There is a continual longing in our hearts. We want something more, but we don't know exactly what that something is.

Jesus knows that our instant contentment in this world will spoil and fade. Jesus knows there is a longing in our hearts that can only be filled in one way. Jesus knows what will ultimately satisfy all our longings, all our hunger pains, all our thirsts, all our desires. Jesus says, "I am the bread of life. He who comes to me will never go hungry, and he who believes in me will never go thirsty" (John 6:35).

No matter how smooth and well things may be going in our lives, and even though we may be thankful how God has blessed us in so many ways—do we realize there is a deeper satisfaction than what we are currently experiencing? There is an aching within our hearts to experience something greater. The answer is not in busying ourselves with more stuff, more ministry or more work. The answer is found in having a greater passion for Jesus. Jesus is urging us to feast upon Him (John 6:53-56). The greater our depth of intimacy and relationship with Jesus, the deeper our satisfaction will be. May we make every effort to become more passionate for Jesus; for he is saying to us: "If anyone is thirsty, let him come to me and drink. Whoever believes in me, as the Scripture has said, streams of living water will flow from within him" (John 7:37-38).

Nowhere Else to Go
John 6:60-69

Continue reflecting upon John 6 in verses 60-69. After Jesus makes His bold proclamation, He loses many followers. In John 6:66 it says, "From this time many of his disciples turned back and no longer followed [Jesus]." However, the Twelve, Jesus' closest disciples, choose to continue following Him. After Jesus asks the Twelve if they want to leave, Peter answers Him by saying, "Lord, to whom shall we go? You have the words of eternal life. We believe and know you are the Holy One of God" (John 6:68-69).

What do we really want out of our lives? Do we desperately want more of Jesus, or do we simply want Jesus to satisfy our every small desire and to bless us in accordance with what we think best? Are we afraid to draw closer to Jesus for fear of what He might call us to do? Would we continue following Him if He told us to do something costly or something which would make us extremely uncomfortable, or would we be ones who turned back as those in John 6:66? Let us be ones who can honestly say with Peter, "Lord, to whom shall we go? You have the words of eternal life. We believe and know you are the Holy One of God" (John 6:68–69).

Jesus Christ, the Son of the Living God, satisfies completely and wholly. He holds the words of life. If you and I do not cling to the words of Jesus, we walk in darkness and death. Who else do we have to go to? Who else holds the words of life? Who or what else can satisfy us completely and wholly? Jesus is the only One. And He immensely desires us to draw close to Him and to hunger and thirst for Him. As we do, He will satisfy us in ways we never before thought possible.

I once heard the following anonymous story, and it illustrates Jesus' desire perfectly:

> There was once a boy who wanted as strong of faith as the old man who took him under his wings to disciple him. The boy asked his mentor, *"How can I be as strong in the faith as you are, and how can I see God do amazing things in my life as you have?"*
>
> The old man then guided the boy out into some water. The boy was a bit nervous because he was unsure what the old man was doing. As they got out into the deep waters, the old man grabbed the boy's head, threw it under the water and held it there. The boy squirmed and thrashed and tried to get his head up in panic. After about fifteen seconds, the boy thought he was going to die. He wanted air so badly, but still the mentor held the boy's head under water. Finally, after a few more seconds passed, the old man let go of the boy's head. The boy shot out of the water, filled his lungs with precious air, and was extremely shocked and confused at what just happened.

The old man then looked sternly into the boys eyes and said, "*Son, when you want the Lord as much as you wanted air just then, only then will you see the Lord move through your life like you never have before.*"

What greater satisfaction is there than what Jesus offers? Oh, that we would long to come to the place in our lives where we never hunger and thirst again; to the place where we yearn for absolute and total peace and rest! For this to happen, our passion must be for Jesus and Jesus alone. The greater our passion for Jesus, the greater our satisfaction will be. Let us pray that our hunger and thirst for Jesus would be superior beyond everything else, even more than for the air we breathe. As this happens, we will begin to be filled and satisfied in ways immeasurable.

The Spirit and the bride say, "Come!" And let him who hears say, "Come!" Whoever is thirsty, let him come; and whoever wishes let him take the free gift of the water of life (Revelation 22:17).

8

Too Much Candy, Too Little Power

"You may not be sure that you want your life to make a difference. Maybe you don't care very much whether you make a lasting difference for the sake of something great. You just want people to like you. If people would just like being around you, you'd be satisfied. Or if you could just have a good job with a good wife, or husband, and a couple of good kids and a nice car and long weekends and a few good friends, a fun retirement, and a quick and easy death, and no hell—if you could have all that (even without God)—you would be satisfied. That is a tragedy in the making. A wasted life."[31]

—John Piper

As you may have noticed, my children provide countless opportunities for illustrations. So let me present another. Living in a small town, my wife and I have been blessed with the opportunity to take our children to various parades where candy is tossed to all the people lined up on the street. If you have ever been to a one of these parades, you know how exciting they are for children. Each child has a bag to put their candy in. The candy is thrown, and all the children scatter picking each piece up. When the parade is over, each child's bag is full of candy, and they are ready to go home—and gorge themselves.

My wife and I usually let our children pick out a few pieces of candy they would like to eat, and then we put the rest on top of the refrigerator. We understand if we put the candy within our children's reach, they very well might eat every piece of it in one sitting. Being the "cruel" parents we are, we tell our children they can have a few pieces of candy for a snack every once in a while, but they need to first eat their meals. If it were up to our children, however, they would choose to skip the meals and eat the candy instead. Through parenting, I have learned that children have an intense desire for candy.

Imagine what would happen if we always let our children have their way. What would happen if we let our children eat nothing but candy for a day? They would feel miserable. What would happen if we let our children eat nothing but candy for a week? They would most likely begin to be sluggish and malnourished. What would happen if we allowed our children to eat nothing but candy for a whole month or more? They could possibly die.

Candy is an extremely poor substitute for nutritional life-sustaining food. Candy may make us feel full, but we cannot survive on candy. Candy offers no nutritional value whatsoever. To survive, our bodies require food that nourishes. Candy may taste really good, be pleasurable, be immediately satisfying and even be filling. But too much candy will make us sick. While candy may give us an immediate satisfaction and may even make us feel full after eating it, in the long run it will not satisfy or sustain us. And if we eat nothing but candy day after day, we will eventually starve to death.

Candy or Vegetables

Back to the verse where Jesus says, "Blessed are those who hunger and thirst for righteousness, for they will be filled" (Matthew 5:6). Again, the filling Jesus is speaking of refers to a complete satisfaction which ultimately leads to true peace. Why then would we allow our desire for anything else to outweigh our desire for the righteousness of God? Only hungering and thirsting for righteousness brings lasting satisfaction and peace, yet so many of us more passionately pursue lesser things than we do the righteousness of God.

Many of us are being deceived. We do not take seriously the truth of 1 Peter 5:9, "Be self-controlled and alert. Your enemy the devil prowls around like a roaring lion looking for someone to devour." Revelation 12:9 speaks about how Satan "deceives the whole world" (NKJV). Though we as believers no longer belong to the world, we are still in this world and can still be deceived by Satan if we are not careful. One of the greatest ways Satan deceives us as believers is by distracting us with the desires of the world, averting our attention away from righteousness, and then convincing us we are still being greatly effective for God's Kingdom. We become like the boy who ate a bag full of candy along with a couple pieces of broccoli and thought he was eating healthy because he ate his vegetables.

Too many people assume that being a Christian is about going to church, serving in a church, knowing the Bible, saying daily prayers, tithing some money and being moral. Yes, these can be virtuous things. But is simply doing these things the sum total of what it means to be a follower of Jesus Christ? Is there more to the Christian life than just these types of things? There is certainly much more.

So many Christians will do all of the things mentioned above, but they will still have a greater desire for the things of the world than for the righteousness of God. Just like the boy who ate the bag full of candy and then ate a couple of vegetables and thought he was eating healthy—many of us are filling our lives with the desires of the world and then doing just enough "Christian things" to ease our conscience and make us feel we are being good Christians.

Think about it. We are able to sit and watch countless hours of television, but we have a hard time sitting and listening to a sermon longer than twenty or thirty minutes. We are able to talk on the phone or sit and chat with our friends for hours on end, but we have a hard time sitting and talking to God in prayer for longer than a few minutes. We will excitedly sit and read the entire newspaper every single morning, but we find it exhausting to sit and read just one chapter of the Bible a day. Many of us as believers do our Christian duty by reading the Bible because we know we need to; praying because we know it is important; going to church because we know it is the Christian thing to do; getting involved in Christian things because that is what noble Christians do; trying "our best" to be an upright and loving Christian in our daily lives. But many of us do these things with about as much joy as we do a chore—just wanting to get it done so we can go do something else more fun.

Something is wrong with this picture. Why are we so bored? Why can't we focus? Why is it so hard to motivate ourselves to seek God? Why are we so apathetic about the things of God? Why do we see such little power in and through our lives? I do not mean to sound harsh but my curiosity is piqued—do the majority of us as Christians truly hunger and thirst for the righteousness of God in our day?

You Can't Have Both

We have all heard the saying, "*You can't have your cake and eat it, too.*" Many of us want the things of this world, yet at the same time want God to fill our lives in amazing ways. In the Parable of the Sower, Jesus describes people who desire both God and the world at the same time: "Still others, like seed sown among thorns, hear the word; but the worries of this life, the deceitfulness of wealth and the desires for other things come in and choke the word, making it unfruitful" (Mark 4:18-19). The gospel of Luke also mentions these same people: "The seed that fell among thorns stands for those who hear, but as they go on their way they are choked by life's worries, riches and pleasures, and they do not mature" (Luke 8:14).

We need to be cautious here. Let us not be tempted to immediately think, "*I am not one who is striving after wealth and worldly desires. I am not filling my life with the worries of this world.*" We must not be too quick to make such a judgment about ourselves. Instead, each of us, as individuals, must examine ourselves thoroughly by asking some difficult but telling questions:

- *Do people regularly tell me they see Jesus through my life, or do they speak of me like they do everyone else?*
- *Is my life causing the people around me to want Jesus more or the things of the world more?*
- *Do I see the fruit of the Holy Spirit greatly increasing in my life, or am I still struggling with the same old sins I have always struggled with?*
- *Do I ever struggle to work more and more to get more money to pay for the things I don't really need even though it hinders my growth in the Lord and the quality of time I spend with my family?*

- *Am I pursuing certain goals because I see how they can glorify God and how He can use them for His purposes, or am I pursuing them because I see how they can benefit me personally?*
- *Do I spend the majority of my money based on what will bring God the most glory, or do I spend my money on whatever I want?*
- *Do I determine how I will spend the majority of my time based simply on how I feel, or by what will be most beneficial for the purposes of God's Kingdom?*
- *Do I see my love and desire for God and my love and compassion for other people increasing in every aspect of my life?*

These are the types of questions you and I need to be asking ourselves as Christians. We must truly examine ourselves in every single area of our lives. We must not be legalistic, but we do need to be discerning of what is right and wrong in everything we do. As we go about our lives, we need to consider such questions as:

- *What will bring God the most glory?*
- *What is the motive of my heart in this?*
- *How will this draw me, and the people around me, closer to Jesus?*
- *Is what I am doing, thinking or saying pleasing to God?*
- *Is the way I am behaving and acting strengthening my own and others faith, hope, trust and love in Jesus Christ?*

As Christians, when our motives are selfish and our desires are worldly we will see very little power in our lives. We cannot have it both ways. Many of us want to see God's power in our lives, but still must admit we desire the things of this world too much. And these worldly desires are choking out the power of the word of God in our lives. Many of us even convince ourselves that the power we are currently experiencing as Christians is for the most part all there is to experience in the Christian life. How often do we as Christians think such things as:

- *I'll never get rid of that sin in my life; that's just the way I am.*
- *I can pray all I want about that, but I am pretty sure it will never happen.*
- *I will never be able to forgive or love that person.*
- *God doesn't heal people anymore.*
- *My church will never change.*
- *That marriage is hopeless.*
- *God doesn't work miracles in our day.*
- *What's the point of gathering and praying with other Christians? Is it really going to change anything?*
- *I know what God's word says, but things just don't work that way in our day.*

Why do we think and believe such things as Christians? Could it be we are arguing from experience and from what we have seen from the majority of churches and Christians' lives around us? Honestly, I have pondered some of these things myself because there simply doesn't seem to be a whole lot of real power coming through the majority of confessing Christians' lives. We so often pray as if we don't really believe our prayers will be answered; talk about people as if they will never change; believe there to be certain sins impossible to overcome; act as if our churches are hopeless; discourage other young Christians from having big visions of what they would like to see God do—as if it were impossible for God to do such things. Without even realizing it, many of us are fulfilling Scripture when it says in the last days there will be those who have a form of godliness but who deny its power (2 Timothy 3:5).

The power of Jesus Christ is greater than many of us realize. The apostle Paul reveals his yearning to know this power as he writes in Philippians 3:10, "I want to know Christ and the power of his resurrection." In regards to this power, I know it is not some superficial power we experience in some gathering. Nor is it simply a power we experience at a single moment in our lives. But, the power God desires for us is real, transformational power in our everyday lives. It is the power of becoming more and more like Jesus Christ in our thinking, our attitude, our actions, our prayers, our authority, and in every other area of our lives. The power God has for us is the same power He used to raise Jesus from the dead (see Romans 8:11).

Some of us may believe there are certain things in our lives that will never come to be. We may say we believe God can do anything, but we often live as if there are certain things He cannot do. We may want to see the power of God unleashed in our lives, but we just feel it will never happen. Many of us may want the peace of God to fill our lives, but peace might be the last thing filling our lives. We may want to experience true rest in Christ and to not be worried or anxious about anything, but that kind of rest may seem nearly impossible for us to enjoy. We may want to be filled by God in amazing ways, but may feel it is not happening as we experience the same old "stuff" day in and day out. We may desire to have a different attitude, but we may continue having the same rotten attitude time and time again.

Whatever it may be, too many Christians are not experiencing the power of God in their lives. Why? It is because we are craving too much "candy." We want to see more of God in our lives and to become more like Jesus, but nothing ever changes because our desire for this world continues to be greater than, or the same, as our passion for the righteousness of God. Therefore we are not being filled as Jesus revealed in Matthew 5:6. And our lack of hungering and thirsting for righteousness is leading to a powerless version of Christianity. On the outside, many of us may look like decent Christians, but a closer look would reveal little or no transformational power emanating from our lives; thus, fulfilling what 2 Timothy 3:5 says about people in the last days—ones "having a form of godliness, but denying its power."

Well Fed Now

In the Old Testament, we see God's lofty warning to Israel about being satisfied by the things of this world. Before the people of Israel enter into the land of God's promise, God cautions them in Deuteronomy 8:10-14,

> When you have eaten and are satisfied, praise the LORD your God for the good land he has given you. Be careful that you do not forget the LORD your God, failing to observe his commands, his laws and his decrees that I am giving you this day. Otherwise, when you eat and are satisfied, when you build fine houses and settle down, and when your herds and flocks grow large and your silver and gold increase and all you have is multiplied, then your heart will become proud and you will forget the LORD your God, who brought you out of Egypt, out of the land of slavery.

We all know what happened next. Israel did indeed forget about the Lord God as they did things their way, ran after everything all the other nations ran after, wanted what all the other nations of the world wanted and filled themselves with every worldly desire. At first, Israel wanted only the Lord but soon they wanted the Lord along with what all the other nations had. They wanted to have their cake and eat it, too. Soon, they found themselves not wanting anything to do with the Lord but living exactly like the people of the world around them. So God gave them over to their worldly desires, and instead of receiving blessing, they began to experience the emptiness and destruction of their worldly desires.

History always has a way of repeating itself. Too many times, we as Christians make the exact same mistakes Israel made. We desperately need to heed to the warnings of God. We must not attempt to satisfy ourselves with any desire of this world. Jesus says in Luke 6:25, "Woe to you who are well fed now, for you will go hungry." Let us be very careful in our want and desire for instant satisfaction in this life. Let us not be like the Israelites who, while in the wilderness, constantly craved for God to meet their immediate needs of food and water; and then once out of the wilderness, greatly desired a king like all the other nations had (see 1 Samuel 8). When God gave the Israelites their fill of these things, they quickly grew fat and happy and forgot about Him. Why? Because their desire for instant satisfaction was greater than their want for God, His will, and His way. If we desire anything more than we do God and His righteousness, God will give us over to these cravings and we will find out just how unfulfilling and destructive these are in truth (see Romans 1:24-27).

The Story of a Haitian

I once heard a testimony from a missionary in Haiti about a certain Christian Haitian man who visited the United States. I cannot remember all of the details of the story, but I can recall the gist of it:

A Haitian man came to the United States, for a month, to visit with some Christians. He enjoyed his visit, but as the month came to an end, and it was time for him to go back to Haiti, someone asked him, *"Are you saddened to have to go back to a life of poverty in Haiti after experiencing the plenty here in the United States?"* The Haitian man replied, *"I must confess that I have greatly enjoyed my time here. The United States has so much to offer. But I am not saddened to be leaving. In the midst of this plenty, I am starting to lose my grip on my faith in God and my desire for Him which I had in the midst of my poverty in Haiti. I am ready to go back to Haiti."*[32]

We Christians in the United States have much to learn from this Haitian man. Why do we so often desire to be safe, comfortable and materially blessed in this life when these things can easily make us lose our grip on our faith in God and our desire for Him? What is it we truly desire?

Our Prayers

The substance of the prayers we pray reveal a lot about what we truly desire. From what I have seen from many different churches, the majority of the prayer concerns have to do with people who are having physical health issues. Also, when we get in groups to pray, often the majority of our prayers have to do with physical ailments for ourselves or for people we know. I must say, it is a good and needful thing to pray for the many different health conditions we face—but is there more we desire than for people to become physically well?

What if we were to examine our own personal prayer lives? When we are alone with God, what are those things which consume our prayers more than any other thing? Do the majority of our prayers have to do with immediate desires in our lives—such things as our finances, our housing situation, our family's comfort and temporary safety, our church's building program, for God to bless everyone and everything in our lives? Don't get me wrong, it is good to pray for all of these things. Actually Scripture tells us: "Do not be anxious about anything, but in everything, by prayer and petition, with thanksgiving, present your requests to God" (Philippians 4:6). However, if all of our requests have to do with our own instant wants, comforts and blessings—what is it we truly desire?

In Chapter 7, the crowd in John 6 was seeking Jesus because they wanted Him to meet an urgent, worldly ambition of theirs. Jesus fed them when they were hungry and so they wanted Jesus to fill another urgent aspiration of theirs—for Jesus to be their king. They thought they knew what was best. But Jesus told them in John 6:26, "I tell you the truth, you are looking for me, not because you saw miraculous signs but because you ate the loaves and had your fill." The crowd did not necessarily want Jesus, but rather they desired for Jesus to do something for them.

What do we want more than any other thing as Christians? If the majority of our prayers consist of asking God to satisfy some instant and worldly want of ours, will we really be wholly satisfied if God gives that want to us? Or would we be satisfied for a moment until we *wanted* something else? What if Jesus has something grander in store for us than just meeting these small desires we *think* we want? What if He is simply waiting for us to ask Him what it is He wants for us instead of what we think is best? Jesus says, "Do not work for food that spoils, but for food that endures to eternal life, which the Son of Man will give you" (John 6:27). Jesus also says, "I am the bread of life. He who comes to me will never go hungry, and he who believes in me will never be thirsty" (John 6:32).

How desperate for Jesus are we? How passionate are we for Him? Is our hunger and thirst for Jesus alone? Does the Spirit groan within us as we pray because we desire Jesus so greatly? What if our passion for the righteousness of God consumed our prayers more than any other thing? What would we see happen in our lives? What kind of power would be unleashed? What depth of peace would we begin to experience?

I wonder what we would begin to experience in our lives if the majority of our prayers were like the prayers we find in Scripture:

- "My soul yearns for you in the night; in the morning my spirit longs for you" (Isaiah 26:9).
- "I spread out my hands to you; my soul thirsts for you like a parched land" (Psalm 143:6).
- "O God, you are my God, earnestly I seek you; my soul thirst for you, my body longs for you, in a dry and weary land where there is no water. I have seen you in the sanctuary and beheld your power and your glory. Because your love is better than life, my lips will glorify you. I will praise you as long as I live, and in your name I will lift up my hands. My soul will be satisfied as with the richest of foods; with singing lips my mouth will praise you" (Psalm 63:1-5).
- "My soul thirsts for the living God. When can I go and meet with him?" (Psalm 42:2).

Do not come away from this section believing I am saying we should never pray for the safety and comfort of our families, for God's blessings, for God to meet our financial needs or for God to provide us with a job. There is a time to pray for all of these things. However, we must carefully consider what it is that consumes the majority of our prayers.

As our passion for Jesus increases our prayers will begin to transform. While we will still pray for our daily needs, we will slowly but surely find ourselves not to be as concerned about these things. Instead, Jesus will begin to become more desirous. Our prayers will begin to shift, revealing our intense desire to know more of Jesus, to grow in our relationship with Him, to be more like Him in every way, to see as He sees, to desire what He desires, to feel as He feels, to see His power displayed in our lives and for Him to fill us in extreme ways.

As our prayers become more focused on Jesus and less focused on our wants, the pure peace of God will begin to flood into our lives. Our prayers will begin becoming more like those found in the Scripture passages. As our passion for the righteousness of God increases our yearning to know God more intimately will be so great that we will actually begin enjoying our time spent with Him in prayer and our time spent reading His word. And as our prayers begin to reveal a desperate yearning for the righteousness of God, Jesus wants us to know: "Blessed are you who hunger now, for you will be satisfied" (Luke 6:21).

9

Craving Come

"The more a true saint loves God with a gracious love, the more he desires to love him, and the more uneasy is he at his want of love to him: the more he hates sin, the more he desires to hate it, and laments that he has so much remaining love to it. The more he mourns for sin, the more he longs to mourn; the more his heart is broken, the more he desires it should be broken. The more he thirsts and longs after God and holiness, the more he longs to long, and breathe out his very soul in longings after God. The kindling and raising of gracious affections is like kindling a flame; the higher it is raised, the more ardent it is; the more it burns, the more vehemently does it tend and seek to burn."[33]

- Jonathan Edwards

In a commentary written by David R. Helm, David shares the following:

The Danish philosopher Søren Kierkegaard tells a parable of the disastrous effects of not putting to death the desires of the flesh, of failing to leave a way of life behind. One springtime a duck was flying with his friends northward across Europe. During the flight he came down in a barnyard where there were tame ducks. He enjoyed some of their corn. He stayed for an hour, and then for a day. One week passed, and before he knew it a month had gone by. He loved the good food, so he stayed all summer long.

One autumn day, when the same wild ducks were winging their way southward again, they passed overhead, and the duck on the ground heard their cries. He was filled with a strange thrill and joy, and he desired to fly with them once again. With a great flapping of wings he rose in the air to rejoin his old comrades in flight.

But he found that his good fare had made him so soft and heavy that he could rise no higher than the eaves of the barn. He dropped back again into the barnyard and said to himself, "*Oh well, my life is safe here, and the food is good.*" Every spring and autumn when he heard the wild ducks honking, his eyes would gleam for a moment, and he would begin flapping his wings. But finally the day came when the wild ducks flew overhead uttering their cries, but he paid no attention. In fact, he failed to hear them at all.[34]

Aspirations

All of us have aspirations. When we are young we dream about all the things we will do when we get older. For example, I remember the days of my college years when God began moving in my heart intensely. I used to go out at night and shout into the heavens prayers like, "*God, use me however You want. Make me a man sold out for Your purposes; one who lives for You and You alone. I want to be dead to myself. I want to please only You. I wonder what You could do through just one person, any person, completely dedicated to You and humbled before You. Oh God, do that through me."*

Though I prayed these types of prayers, I must admit that my life was not completely in order. Honestly, I still struggled with all sorts of sins. And understanding this as a problem, I was desperate for God to change me and use me. I yearned for something more out of life; more than just the same old, same old. I did not want to be just another statistic of an American Christian who looked more like the world around him than like Jesus Christ. I yearned for the sins I struggled with to be gone once and for all; longed to know God's word in a deeper way; thirsted for more of God's power in my life; hungered deeply to know Jesus in complete truth regardless of the costs. I didn't want to just fit into the Christian crowd, but wanted to move further and allow God to do things in and through me that I never before dreamed possible. I remember craving God so much in my college days that, in reality, I just wanted to be with Him in Heaven. My heart beat for eternity.

Now, I could go into great detail about how God has worked in my life since my time in college, but that would take a whole other book. Let me just say that it has been about fourteen years since I began praying prayers like those in college and God has been transforming my life, my thinking, my passion, my feelings, my desires and my everything in absolutely amazing ways. In no way am I perfect. I still fall into sin at times. I still sometimes think things that I should not. I still do stupid things and then think, *"Why in the world did I do that?"*

However, there are things I used to struggle with that I no longer do. When I think back to the way I used to think, I can honestly say my thoughts are more pure than they used to be. When I consider the things I used to entertain myself with and find pleasure in, I no longer find many of those things to be entertaining or pleasurable.

Please, do not misunderstand. In no way am I boasting about myself or about how good I am. The message is this: I am seeing the power of God transforming me as a new creature in Christ Jesus—a creature I could never make myself into. What I love and the way I love is changing. What I enjoy is changing. How I spend my time is changing. My love for God's word is growing. My desire to know God is increasing. And I trust, as I continue to hunger and thirst for God and His righteousness, God's transformational power will increase in and through my life, which will lead me to a deeper and deeper experience of the peace and rest of God.

As I continue to seek the Lord, He *will* fill me more and more. And trust me, there is much more work to be done in and through me! When I think I am really getting somewhere in this maturity process of my faith, God reveals *more* sin deep within this old heart of mine. God is cleansing and purifying me. And though it is clear to me that much more needs to be transformed and cleansed within me, the exciting part is that I actually see it happening. My faith in Jesus Christ is not just making me *feel* better, but it is actually transforming everything about me. There is a power in me greater than I could ever make up myself. The power of Jesus Christ within me is—REAL. And now that I have tasted of the "power of the resurrection," (Philippians 3:10) I cannot wait to see what else God has to do in and through the rest of my life.

I share all of this simply to give hope. If God can take someone like me and transform me as He is, He can do the exact same thing in anybody's life. But know that this power of God is unleashed through hungering and thirsting for Him and His righteousness. As Jesus says, "Blessed are those who hunger and thirst for righteousness, for they will be filled" (Matthew 5:6).

Break the Cycle

Think about the story of the duck at the beginning of this chapter. I share this story because it reminds me of what is happening in much of the Christian culture in the United States. So many Christians have sat back and grown comfortable in the world for so long that they have forgotten who it is God desires them to be. Like the wild duck in the story who eventually did not pay any attention to the other wild ducks flying over-head, many Christians may see other believers who are on fire for God, yet be unmoved by those people's passion because they are so captivated and distracted by their own worldly affairs and business matters. The wild duck did not belong on the farm, but he was content and comfortable on the farm. He even grew too fat and soft to fly with his wild duck buddies.

In a similar way, too many believers have fattened and softened themselves with the things of the world and cannot seem to get their feet off the ground to experience the power of God in their lives. Many people may see other Christians displaying the power of God, but then find that they themselves have become so fattened by the world, in a spiritual sense, and so sucked into the sinful gratifications of the world that they think it impossible to see the transformational power of God displayed in their own lives and in the lives of their families.

Some believers truly do desire to see God's power displayed in their lives but feel like they cannot break the cycle in which they find themselves. Maybe there are times when they get excited about God, read His word regularly and pray more frequently. During these times, they might go and joyfully share with others how the Lord is working in their lives. And then, what seems out of nowhere, they fall back into an old way of life and go backwards in their spiritual journey. Maybe they fall back into an old sin. Maybe they slip back into depression. Maybe they get busy as their daily chores consume them, dampening their desire for the Lord. As time goes by, they think, "*What am I doing? I need to surrender my life back over to the Lord.*" And so they do, for a while, until they fall back to their old ways again. And the cycle continues.

If Satan can keep us Christians stuck in this type of cycle, he can keep us from being effective for God's purposes. But we must be convinced of this extremely important truth—*the cycle can be broken!* So many times we try to break this cycle by going to spiritual conferences or seminars to get fired up in our faith. And we do get a charge. But then we go back to the daily routine and grind of life and our fire and passion dies again. Soon we don't feel much of God's power at work in our lives anymore and we begin to think, "*I need to go to another conference to get charged up again.*" Why does our passion so quickly fade? Why can't we keep the fire within our hearts? If our passion for God's righteousness continually fades and needs sparked over and over again like this, we need more than a conference or seminar to renew our passion. This cycle must be broken—once and for all.

I have heard so many Christians say things like:

- *I'll never see God move through my life like that person.*
- *I just feel so helpless and distracted. I want to see God move through my life in awesome ways, but then I constantly busy myself; doing those things I know I should not do.*
- *I would like to be passionately on fire for God at all times in my life, but I just don't see any way for that to be possible.*

We may be able to relate to one of these statements and truly wonder how we can be a person continually passionate for the Lord, seeing God's power at work in and through our lives on a daily basis. Possibly we are at a point in our lives where we are sick and tired of the status quo and we want to know God and His power in a way like we've never known before. We want our passion for Jesus to remain red hot, never again to grow cold. Do we believe this is possible?

A Night with My Son

I have been a pastor of a church for nearly six years now. The Lord called me into the ministry to preach and teach the truths of His word to the church, to build disciples and to show love and compassion toward His people. But a few years ago, I began feeling myself simply going through the motions of being a pastor. Preparing sermons and Bible studies started to become more of a duty than a joy. Reading the Bible became a daily chore. My prayers felt weak and distracted. I felt my desire and passion for the Lord slowly fading. Alarm bells began ringing within my spirit. Something was wrong—I was beginning to grow cold in my faith.

For the most part, I'm the kind of guy who is quiet when it comes to my own personal matters. So, on the outside you may never have known what was really happening in my life. I must confess, pastors can sometimes put on a "godly act" and I guess that's what I was doing. But, I knew my desire for God was fading. One day, while visiting a friend, I ran across a book with some testimonies from the life of men like John Wesley, Charles Finney and Duncan Campbell. These men experienced the power of God in ways many of us have never witnessed before. As I read the testimonies of these men, I began wondering: "*Why are so many of us not seeing God move in and through our churches and our own personal lives as these men did? Why am I not seeing God's power displayed through my own life as these men did?"* Although God has indeed done much through my life and I have seen Him work in many amazing ways, during this dry spell, I wanted to see so much more of God and His power than I was currently experiencing.

For weeks I began praying hard and considering how God's power is to be unleashed without restraint in a person's life. One morning while praying about my desire to be as passionate for the Lord as the men I was reading about, I fell flat on my face and heard God whisper to my heart, *"How much do you truly desire Me, Adam?"* At that moment I knew the Lord was calling me to a fast from food for seven days. The longest I ever fasted from food before that was three days, and honestly I didn't enjoy it. I wasn't all that excited about a seven day fast either. But I knew through this fast, God had something to teach me about desiring Him more than anything. So I fasted for seven days.

A few weeks after the fast, something extraordinary happened to me. It was a summer night around midnight and my wife and I had not been asleep very long before we heard our son, Gabriel, who was two years old at the time, start crying. We got up to see why he was crying and could tell he was just over tired from staying up too late that night. Since he was having trouble sleeping, he chose to respond by screaming and crying. We tried calming him through patting his back, getting him a drink of water, rocking him—but all our efforts were in vain. He began crying out and screaming even more loudly and uncontrollably. This went on for the next two hours. My compassion began to fade. I was tired and irritable, and I just wanted him to go to sleep so *I* could go to sleep.

About two o'clock in the morning, as I was lying in bed listening to the over-tired screams of my son, I felt the Lord whisper to my heart, *"Adam, go pray over your son."* Immediately, I got up and went to kneel at the foot of my son's bed and began to pray. Gabriel did not know I was in the room because he was in a "half-asleep-half-awake" mode and had his eyes shut while crying. But as soon as I knelt down and began to pray, he stopped crying. At first I thought this was merely coincidence and that he would start crying at any moment. He didn't. So, I kept praying. My son drifted off to sleep. After kneeling there for about ten minutes, I heard the Lord whisper to me, *"Adam, I used your son's crying to get you out of bed and bring you to your knees in prayer."*

My son stopped crying that night, but the Lord kept me in prayer. I knelt there until about four o'clock in the morning. During this early morning prayer session, the Lord's presence came upon me in a way like never before. Here is what I wrote in my prayer journal the next morning:

> Gabriel was screaming since 12:30 am and I felt I was going to go crazy. Nothing would calm him. I rocked him for about twenty minutes but still he whined and screamed and cried. I grew so angry! Yet the verse, "love is patient" (1 Corinthians 13:4) kept going through my mind. At about 2:30 am I felt led to go pray in his room to calm him down. So with him still crying and not going to sleep, I knelt down at the end of his bed and began praying, and immediately he stopped. I prayed there for over an hour and he slept. Thank You Lord! And in the midst of prayer, I felt the Holy Spirit come upon me in a way as never before. You, Oh God, allowed me get a glimpse of Your heart, to feel as You feel, and for the first time in a long time I wept, tears and all. It was not made up or forced, but I wept for the church and for all of those who seem so powerless to do anything. I prayed for more power; an unleashing of the Holy Spirit. I prayed with

such earnestness as I've never prayed before. And I didn't even feel tired the whole time. You yearn for people to know You, You love them so much. You so want them to turn to You. I prayed over and over again about how we are so helpless and powerless without You and how we are in such great need of You. I prayed for a new anointing and refreshing. I strongly sensed that You are up to something great, right here in my church and in this area, and You are bringing me to the place to feel it. Well, I went to bed at 3:40 am. Gabriel cried once more after that but then went right back to sleep. Thank You, Lord, for this experience. I felt Your presence and nearness so strongly! It was a tender time, so loving and sweet. I just wanted to stay there, to run away and talk with You, to sit down with some coffee and just have You speak to me. But I felt as if around 3:40 am I started to lose focus as weariness came upon me. Yet, still, I hated to come out of that time; so sweet, so powerful, so true, so real.

God used that summer night to reveal His heart to me in a way I never felt or experienced before. He gave me a glimpse of how He feels. And now I realize—feeling God's heart is a whole lot different than just knowing about God's heart. God immensely desires His people to feel as He feels, long as He longs, see as He sees, love as He loves.

Through this journey of desiring to see more of God's power unleashed in and through my life, God is continually teaching me that the amount of His power displayed in and through my life is closely connected to the depth of my passion for Him and His righteousness. I know I keep repeating Matthew 5:6 over and over again, but this is the one verse God keeps putting upon my own heart: "Blessed are those who hunger and thirst for righteousness, for they will be filled." I am beginning to understand—the greater my hunger and thirst for righteousness, the greater the overflow of God's power in my life.

God has such a deep desire for His people to yearn for Him and His righteousness. When we desire for God to reveal His power to us, He will begin to open our eyes to how His power is unleashed—through passion for His righteousness. Yet, we must understand that we cannot stir up a passion within our hearts that doesn't exist. Only God can bring us to the point where He wants us to be. We must only ask Him to bring us to this point. If we ask, He will answer. And as we seek the Lord and ask Him to intensify our passion for His righteousness, our desire will continue to increase. Jesus says in Matthew 6:33, "But seek first his kingdom and his righteousness." And in Matthew 7:7-11,

> Ask and it will be given to you; seek and you will find; knock and the door will be opened to you. For everyone who asks receives; he who seeks finds; and to him who knocks, the door will be opened.
>
> Which of you, if his son asks for bread, will give him a stone? Or if he asks for a fish, will give him a snake? If you, then, though you are evil, know how to give good gifts to your children, how much more will your Father in heaven give good gifts to those who ask him!

Pray for Your Craving to Come

God wants us to crave Him and His righteousness more than any other thing. We might say, "*I want to be passionate for the Lord, but honestly, I am simply not that passionate. I can't force myself to feel something I don't feel, nor do I want to.*" With that reality, let us be emboldened in doing a few things:

Pray Honestly

Honesty before God is of utmost importance. Psalm 101:7 reveals, "No one who practices deceit will dwell in my house; no one who speaks falsely will stand in my presence." Proverbs 12:22 states, "The LORD detests lying lips, but he delights in men who are truthful." Many of us would not consider ourselves as liars. We may even do our best to speak truthfully and never intentionally lie to other people. But when it comes to our prayer lives—how many of us make an intentional effort to always pray honestly?

In considering our prayers, we must each confess there have been too many times we have simply gone through the motions of prayer. Routinely praying for all those things we know we should without giving much thought to what we are praying for. When praying in public, simply spitting off the right prayer lingo and caring more about how our prayers sound in other people's ears and less about the heart of our prayers. When praying privately, simply going through our prayer lists rather boringly and casually praying that God be glorified in our lives; for God to bring salvation to people; for God to make a sick person well; for God to bless our nation; for God's will to be done. And doing this simply because we know that these are the types of things we are supposed to be praying for as "good" Christians. How often do we think that if we say all the right words in our prayers we have done our job as God's prayer warriors?

Each of us would have to admit that we have done and still do these very things at times in our prayers. But God wants us to understand an important truth—we should always be honest and heartfelt in our prayers. If we do not really feel like praying, we need to express this to God. If there is something that is really bothering us, we need to specifically pray about this. If we are struggling with something, we need to tell this to God. If there is a specific and continual sin in our lives, we need to honestly talk to God about our struggle. God wants us to be honest with Him.

Honesty and humility go hand in hand. How many times do we assume something about ourselves to be true which, in reality, is not true; specifically when it comes to our love, desire and devotion for God? Sometimes we may think ourselves more spiritually mature than we ought. Many of us deceivingly convince ourselves we are a strong person of faith and that God is the most important aspect of our lives even if in reality that is not true. Many of us refuse to see our hearts as God sees our hearts, but rather put on a false pretense to convince others and ourselves that we truly are ones who hunger and thirst for the righteousness of God. In Luke 18:10-14 Jesus gives a story:

> Two men went up to the temple to pray, one a Pharisee and the other a tax collector. The Pharisee stood up and prayed about himself: "God, I thank you that I am not like other men—robbers, evildoers, adulterers—or even like this tax collector. I fast twice a week and give a tenth of all I get."
>
> But the tax collector stood at a distance. He would not even look up to heaven, but beat his breast and said, "God, have mercy on me, a sinner."
>
> I tell you that this man, rather than the other, went home justified before God. For everyone who exalts himself will be humbled, and he who humbles himself will be exalted.

Pretending to be a strong person of faith, if we truly are not, is powerless and sinful. We must be careful not to deceive ourselves in believing a lie. We desperately need to be honest with ourselves, and more importantly, with God. Revelation 3:17-18 provides a strong warning to the lukewarm church in Laodicia:

> You say, "I am rich; I have acquired wealth and do not need
> a thing." But you do not realize that you are wretched,
> pitiful, poor, blind and naked. I counsel you to buy from
> me gold refined in the fire, so you can become rich; and
> white clothes to wear, so you can cover your shameful
> nakedness; and salve to put on your eyes, so you can see.

Many of us need to urgently heed to this warning given to the Laodicians. We must be extremely cautious in simply assuming we are being the people God desires us to be and living in the fullness Jesus calls us to. Because it is quite possible that a closer look may reveal otherwise. God is calling us to perform a true evaluation of our hearts and lives.

If each of us as individuals were to honestly look at our lives, could we rightly say we are more passionate for God and His righteousness than any other thing? If not, then we must go straight to God and tell Him. Honesty before God means we readily admit to Him—when we struggle to keep Him the center of our lives; when we become bored at reading Scripture and praying; when we don't feel like loving someone; when we fall into a specific sin; how we truly want to change but feel powerless to do so.

There may be times when we feel passionate for God; then other times we do not. We must share this with the Lord in prayer, and confess to Him that we cannot force ourselves to become something we are not. He has to be the One who works within our hearts to do what we, ourselves, cannot do. God already knows our hearts. He knows whether we truly hunger and thirst for righteousness. We may be able to discipline ourselves to be a spiritual person on the outside, but only God can radically transform our hearts so that we begin feeling as He feels and seeing as He sees. God wants us to be honest in our prayers, to admit where we are. He is urgently calling us to humbly ask Him to increase our passion for His righteousness.

Boldly Ask for What You Know God Wants

In Luke 11:1-13 Jesus is discussing prayer and how we are to pray as believers. In verses 5-8 Jesus provides a story, showing how He wants us to pray:

> Suppose one of you has a friend, and he goes to him at midnight and says, "Friend, lend me three loaves of bread, because a friend of mine on a journey has come to me, and I have nothing to set before him."
>
> Then the one on the inside answers, "Don't bother me. The door is already locked, and my children are with me in bed. I can't get up and give you anything." I tell you, though he will not get up and give him the bread because he is his friend, yet because of the man's boldness he will get up and give him as much as he needs (Luke 11:5-8).

Sparing the details of why this man needed bread at midnight, simply recognize that this man was obviously in desperate need of bread since he was willing to go to his neighbor's house at midnight. And because of the man's boldness, his neighbor gave him the bread he needed. Jesus' point could not be clearer—we, as God's children, are to come to the throne of God boldly with our requests. And when we are certain what God desires of us, we ought to be even bolder in our prayers.

God wants us to be passionate for His righteousness. We must be earnest; boldly asking God to fill us with a greater hunger and thirst for Him. Let us come before God and ask Him confidently for greater passion. We, who are in Christ, have nothing to fear. God is our Father, and He is perfectly good.

Persevere to the Point of Breakthrough

After Jesus tells the story of the bold man in Luke 11:5-8, He continues in verses 9-11,

> So I say to you: Ask and it will be given to you; seek and you will find; knock and the door will be opened to you. For everyone who asks receives; he who seeks finds; and to him who knocks, the door will be opened (Luke 11:9-11).

When we begin praying for those things we already know God desires for us, we will begin to experience the answering of our prayers. The answers may not come overnight, but they will be answered. We must only persevere.

In the tenth chapter of the book of Daniel, Daniel is given a revelation. Daniel is so bothered by the vision that he begins three weeks of fasting, praying and mourning. He never gives up. Daniel perseveres until he receives an answer to his prayers. After the three weeks are over, a messenger comes to Daniel, giving the answer he has been looking for:

> Do not be afraid, Daniel. Since the first day that you set your mind to gain understanding and to humble yourself before your God, your words were heard, and I have

come in response to them. But the prince of the Persian kingdom resisted me twenty-one days. Then Michael, one of the chief princes, came to help me, because I was detained there with the king of Persia. Now I have come to explain to you what will happen to your people in the future, for the vision concerns a time yet to come.

As we pray for an increase of passion for God's righteousness in our lives, we must persevere until our answer comes. We must know that "our struggle is not against flesh and blood, but against the rulers, against the authorities, against the powers of this dark world and against the spiritual forces of evil in the heavenly realms" (Ephesians 6:12). There is a spiritual battle warring around us which our physical eyes cannot see. The enemy does not want our hunger and thirst for God's righteousness to increase, because he knows the power of God which will be unleashed in our lives. This is why we must persevere, in prayer, for passion in our lives. We must pray and never give up. If we do, our prayers will be answered. Proverbs 10:24 makes it very clear, "What the righteous desire will be granted."

In Psalm 37:4 it says, "Delight yourself in the Lord and He will give you the desires of your heart." If we are delighting ourselves in the Lord, then we will begin to desire what He desires of us. This is why our passion for His righteousness must increase. Because as it does, we will begin to want what He wants, and for this reason He will truly give us the desires of our hearts. As we delight ourselves in the Lord, increasing in our passion for His righteousness, we will experience the power and peace of God in ways immeasurable.

Let us pray for a greater passion for God in our lives and not give up; pressing in for an increase of passion. One day we will experience breakthrough. It may not happen overnight. It may not happen very quickly at all. But if we persevere, we will slowly but surely witness an increase of God's power displayed through our lives. As this happens, we will be flooded with the peace of God which transcends all understanding. This is the Christian life Jesus intends for us to experience, the type of life that brings God the most glory.

As the Apostle Paul

"For to me, to live is Christ and to die is gain" (Philippians 1:21). This is a statement of a man who hungered and thirsted for the righteousness of God. Paul wanted nothing other than Jesus Christ, the Righteous One. Everything about Paul's life was about Jesus Christ. Living or dying didn't matter to him. If Paul continued to live, he would live in the power of Christ. If he died, he would be with Christ. Paul wanted only Jesus. He hungered and thirsted for Jesus alone; to know Him and to experience the power of His resurrection (Philippians 3:10).

For you who are reading this book, I pray for an increasing of passion for Jesus, the Righteous One, in your life. I pray for a deepening in your relationship with Jesus Christ and for you to fully grasp that knowing Him is all that matters. There is no secret formula to follow to see God's power in your life; it has to do with the depth of your relationship with Jesus Christ. Draw closer to Christ and seek to know Him. Only then will your passion grow immensely. And as your passion for the righteousness of God increases, you will one day see a massive unleashing of God's power manifested in and through your life. You will then begin to understand the true peace and rest which only Jesus can give. Grow in YOUR PASSION and be filled with GOD'S POWER!

"Blessed are those who hunger and thirst
for righteousness, for they will be filled."
– Matthew 5:6

"Almighty God, make us a people who hunger and thirst for Your righteousness. Let our passion never fade. Fill us with everything You are. Let us experience the life only Jesus can bring. We are in such great need of You. We are so weak in and of ourselves. Fill us with passion. Show us Your Power. In Jesus' Name, Amen."

"What is wrong with Christians in our day is that they have the gifts of God but have forgotten the God of the gifts. There is a difference between noble, strong, vigorous and satisfying spiritual experience and the other kind of spiritual experience, which takes the gifts of God but forgets the Giver."[35]

– A. W. Tozer

Listen to Pastor Adam's Sermons Online at:

www.sermon.net/adammeisberger

Contact Adam at:

adammeisberger@yahoo.com

NOTES

1   Wesley L. Duewel, *Ablaze for God* (Grand Rapids, Michagan: Zondervan Publishing House, 1989), 29.

Introduction: More to this Life

2   A.W. Tozer, *Experiencing the Presence of God: Teachings From the Book of Hebrews* (California: Regal, 2010), 135.

3   I fully understand that this statement is easier to *say* than to actually *live out* when things in our lives seem to be crumbling. But that doesn't change the fact that we still must do this as Christians, as James 1:2 says, *"Consider it pure joy, my brothers, whenever you face trials of many kinds."*

4   For one example see: Barna Group, *Faith Has a Limited Behavior On Most People's Behavior*, accessed April 18, 2013, http://www.barna.org/barna-update/article/5-barna-update/188-faith-has-a-limited-effect-on-most-peoples-behavior.

5   Homiletics Online, *The Church and the Mosaic Generation*, accessed April 18, 2013, http://www.homileticsonline.com/subscriber/interviews/barna.asp

6   Christian Today, *Study Compares Christian and Non-Christian Lifestyles*, accessed April 18, 2013, http://www.christiantoday.com/article/american.study. reveals.indulgent.lifestyle.christians.no.different/9439-2.htm.

7   2 Timothy 3:5

Chapter 1: Desperate for Water and Food

8   Duewel, *Ablaze for God*, 31.

9   The concept of "thirsting", at least in my own mind, carries more weight than the term "hungering". Hunger is defined as "any strong desire". Thirst, however, is defined more intensely by the word "craving". True, the terms "hunger" and "thirst" are words that carry nearly the same idea and can be used almost simultaneously, but at least in my own mind, the term "thirst" carries more intensity than does the term "hunger".

10 "Hunger," *Webster's New World Dictionary, Third Collage Edition* (Massachusetts, Houghton Mifflin Company, 1995).

11 "Thirst," *Webster's New World Dictionay.*

Chapter 2: Our One Passion Revealed

12 D. L. Moody, *Weighed and Wanting: Addresses on the Ten Commandments* (Chicago, New York, Toronto: Fleming H. Revell Company, 1898), accessed March 15, 2013, http://articles.ochristian.com/article18039.shtml.

13 "Passion," *Webster's New World Dictionary.*

Chapter 3: Get This Right

14 R. A. Torrey, *Why God Used D. L. Moody* (Philadelphia: Fleming H. Revell Company, 1923), accessed March 15, 2013, http://www.whatsaiththe scripture.com/Voice/Why.God.Used.D.L.Moody. html.

15 Jesus says in John 15:7-8, "*If you remain in me and my words remain in you, ask whatever you wish, and it will be given you. This is to my Father's glory, that you bear much fruit, showing yourselves to be my disciples.*" We are to remain close to Jesus, and even more, we are to actually remain in Him. As we remain in Jesus and in His words, real life and power begin to be displayed in our lives, which is the fruit that reveals us to be a true disciple of Jesus.

Chapter 4: Desiring Righteousness: Part I

[16] E. M. Bounds, *Power through Prayer* (Grand Rapids, Michigan: Christian Classics Ethereal Library) accessed April 2, 2013, http://www.ccel.org/ ccel /bounds/power.pdf.

Chapter 5: Desiring Righteousness: Part II

[17] Jonathan Edwards, "On Religious Affections," Section XI, *The Works of Jonathan Edwards*, Volume 1 (Peabody, Massachusetts: Hendrickson, 2004), 314.

[18] See Romans 3

[19] Isaiah 63:1

[20] G. Kittel and G.W. Bromiley and G. Friedrich, ed., *Vol. 4: Theological dictionary of the New Testament* (Grand Rapids, MI: Eerdmans, 1964), electronic edition.

Chapter 6: You Will Be Filled

[21] Charles H. Spurgeon, *The Treasury of David*, accessed March 15, 2013, http://www.spurgeon.org/treasury/ps042.htm.

[22] J. Swanson. *Dictionary of Biblical Languages with Semantic Domains: Greek New Testament* (Oak Harbor: Logos Research Systems, Inc., 1997), electronic edition.

[23] M.R. Vincent, *Word studies in the New Testament* (New York: Charles Scribner's Sons, 1887), electronic edition.

[24] Romans 8:8 makes it very clear that "*if anyone does not have the Spirit of Christ, he does not belong to Christ.*" We either have God's Spirit living in us, or we do not. If we do not have God's Spirit living in us, then we truly are not Christian, even if we *think* we are. Romans 8:16 mentions, "*The Spirit testifies with our spirit that we are God's children.*"

[25] See Ephesians 6:10–18 and 1 Peter 5:8-9.

[26] Randy Alcorn, *Heaven*, (Wheaton, Illinois: Tyndale House, 2004), 454-455.

[27] J. Swanson, *Dictionary of Biblical Languages with Semantic Domains: Hebrew Old Testament* (Oak Harbor: Logos Research Systems, Inc., 1997), electronic edition.

[28] Ibid.

[29] Ibid.

Chapter 7: Eternally Satisfied

[30] John Wesley, *Sermon 93 On Redeeming the Time*, accessed April 2, 2013, http://www.ccel.org/ccel/wesley/sermons.vi.xl.html

Chapter 8: Too Much Candy, Too Little Power

[31] John Piper, Don't Waste Your Life, (Wheaton, IL: Crossway Books, 2007), 45.

[32] Anonymous.

Chapter 9: Craving Come

[33] Edwards, "On Religious Affections," 312.

[34] David R. Helm, *1 & 2 Peter and Jude*, (Wheaton, IL: Crossway Books, 2008), 131.

[35] A. W. Tozer, *Living as a Christian* (Ventura, California: Regal, 2009), 93-94.

CPSIA information can be obtained at www.ICGtesting.com
Printed in the USA
BVOW04s1649270913

332323BV00002B/2/P